KATHRYN LASKY
TRACES OF LIFE
THE ORIGINS OF HUMANKIND

ILLUSTRATED BY

WHITNEY POWELL

MORROW JUNIOR BOOKS / NEW YORK

For our friend Fran Silverman
K.L. & W.P.

ACKNOWLEDGMENTS

The author and illustrator thank Dr. David Pilbeam of the Department of Anthropology, Harvard University; Dr. Robert L. Dorit, Department of Biology, Harvard University; and Dr. Rick Potts, Curator of Anthropology, Smithsonian Institution, for their careful readings of this work.

Permission for photographs is gratefully acknowledged: American Museum of Natural History, courtesy Department Library Services: pp. 6 (Neg. #39666), 32 (Neg. #326697), 69 (Neg. #109353); K. Cannon-Bonventre/Anthro Photo: p. 66; Field Museum of Natural History and the artist Frederick Blaschke, Chicago: p. 115 (Neg. #66834); Dr. David Pilbeam: p. 46; John Reader/Science Photo Library: p. 55; UPI/Bettmann Newsphotos: p. 89.

1 2 3 4 5 6 7 8 9 10
Library of Congress Cataloging-in-Publication Data
Lasky, Kathryn.
Traces of life : the origins of humankind/Kathryn Lasky;
illustrations by Whitney Powell.
p. cm.
Bibliography: p.
Includes index.
Summary: Discusses research and theories concerning the earliest human beings.
ISBN 0-688-07237-2.
1. Human evolution—Juvenile literature. [1. Man—Origin.
2. Evolution. 3. Man, Prehistoric.] I. Powell, Whitney, ill.
II. Title.
GN281.L36 1989
573.2—dc20 89-12092 CIP AC

Contents

Seventy-five Seconds Before Midnight

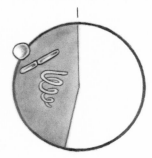

MIDNIGHT TO NOON

MICROORGANISMS

Time can become unimaginable. The earth is almost five billion years old. If we were to make a twenty-four-hour clock, each hour equal to 200 million years, and pretend that the earth had come into being at exactly midnight on, say, a Monday, it would not be until nearly dawn that the first life would appear.

Bacteria were among the first living organisms. Hundreds of thousands can fit easily on the head of a pin. Despite their small dimensions they come in a variety of shapes—spheres, rods, and spirals. They grew to make

4

MIDNIGHT TO NOON

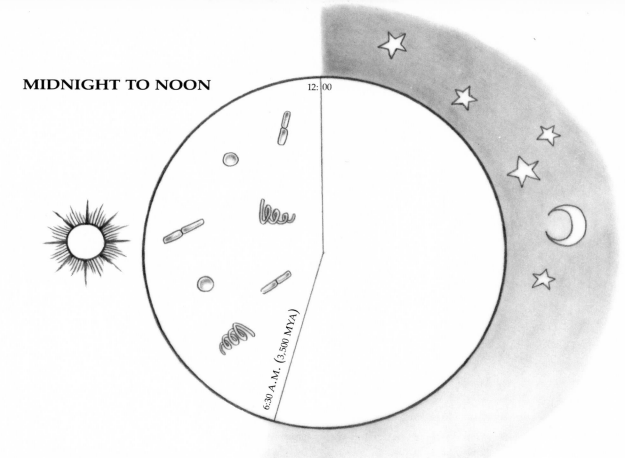

6:30 A.M. (3,500 MYA)

12:00

MYA = MILLIONS OF YEARS AGO

NOON TO MIDNIGHT

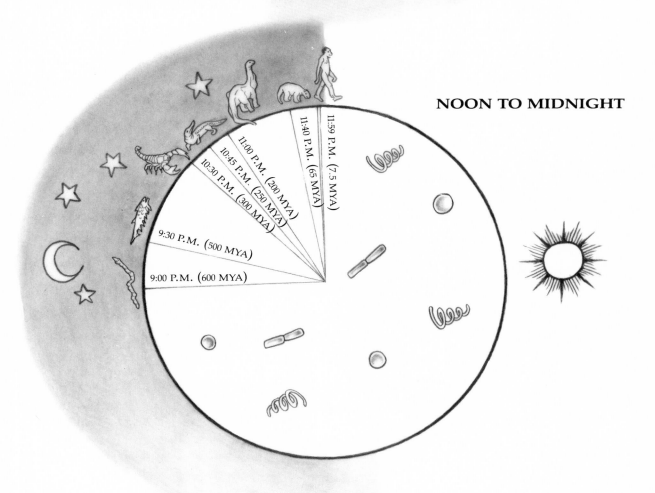

11:59 P.M. (7.5 MYA)

11:40 P.M. (65 MYA)

11:00 P.M. (200 MYA)

10:45 P.M. (250 MYA)

10:30 P.M. (300 MYA)

9:30 P.M. (500 MYA)

9:00 P.M. (600 MYA)

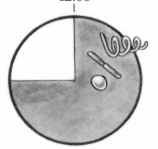

MICROORGANISMS

Microorganisms are the only life.

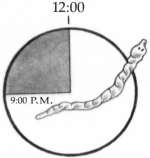

9:00 P.M.

CAMBRIAN
EXPLOSION

Some creatures from the Cambrian Explosion continue to live today.

Opabina

those earliest forms of life we call *algae*—leafless, rootless plants that floated on water. Their presence three and a half billion years ago has been confirmed in the traceries they left on ancient rock. These rock traceries are one kind of fossil.

From dawn, when those first algae floated in calm tidal pools, into the morning, through an afternoon, and well into the evening—or another three billion years on our clock—no life other than these microorganisms would exist.

Then, at 9:00 P.M., something happened. There was a burst of new life that we call the Cambrian Explosion. There were more new life forms than a single person could count—had a single person been around, which was not the case. There were all sorts of jellyfish, sponges, mollusks (like clams or snails), creatures similar to crabs and shrimp—and there were worms. Many worms! Not one of these animals had a backbone, although some had shells. None of these animals ran or leaped or roared for food. They lived in water or mud and they were all really small. An animal eight inches long was considered gigantic by Cambrian standards. Many of them have been given wonderful-sounding names. Wixwaxia was a wormish creature. Hallucigenia, tube-shaped with a spade-shaped head, was supported by seven pairs of toothpick-like legs. Opabina had a fat slug-shaped body with a head at one end that sported five mushroom-like "eyes." These creatures no longer exist in living form. They became *extinct*. To become extinct does not mean to die as an individual organism dies, but rather to die out forever as a *species* so that no descendants are left to carry on the line. Some organisms, such as clams and snails and certain kinds of jellyfish, lived on.

The Cambrian Explosion began 600 million years ago. It lasted over 100 million years. Back then, we hardly would have recognized the earth. On a globe, the continents of the world look something like jigsaw pieces. Hundreds of millions of years ago, many fitted together into solid masses. Over time they broke apart, drifted, collided, sank, and resurfaced.

During the Cambrian Explosion what we now call the "landlocked" midwest of the United States was awash. From Pennsylvania to Utah the water was chest-high. You could have dived for sea urchins in Indianapolis and gathered clams in Cleveland. But the earth's crust, or outer covering, is brittle and can break when powerful forces underneath it push out. About 400 million years ago, there was a bulge and a snap in the ocean floor. Steam and *magma*, the molten rock deep within the earth, spurted from the crack and formed a new oceanic crust of material. The ocean floor, newly crusted, began to spread, giving anything in its path a shove. The landmass that is now North America was in its path, and it was shoved upward. It started to drain and become greener and to welcome new life on land.

North America was not the only continent being shoved around. Nothing on the earth stands still. The poles have slid. Even the equator has moved. Two hundred million years ago North America, South America, Greenland, India, Australia, Africa, Madagascar, and Antarctica were joined together into one huge continental mass called Pangea. One hundred thirty-five million years ago, Pangea began to break apart, causing many dramatic changes. India drifted north and collided with mainland Asia. The impact of the collision formed the Himalayan mountains. Madagascar was still attached to East Africa, and South

7

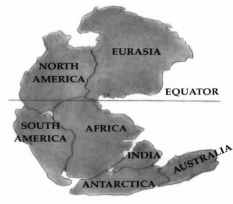

200 MYA

135 MYA

70 MYA

PRESENT

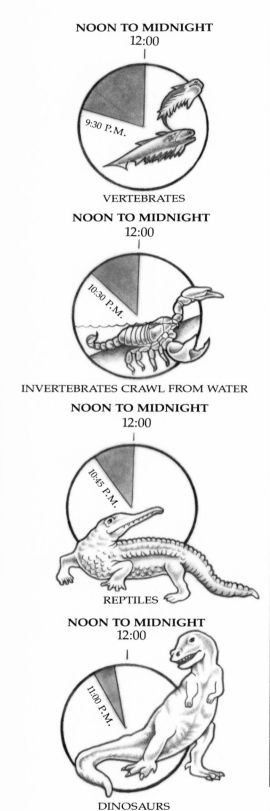

NOON TO MIDNIGHT
12:00

9:30 P.M.

VERTEBRATES

NOON TO MIDNIGHT
12:00

10:30 P.M.

INVERTEBRATES CRAWL FROM WATER

NOON TO MIDNIGHT
12:00

10:45 P.M.

REPTILES

NOON TO MIDNIGHT
12:00

11:00 P.M.

DINOSAURS

America was still connected to Africa. It would be millions of years before the globe looked anything like we now know it, and it is still on the move!

The Cambrian Explosion lasted a half hour on our imaginary clock. At about 9:30 came the first *vertebrates*—fish with backbones. A few minutes later, a greenness could be seen at the water's edge as tiny leafless plants began to float from the sea and grow on the barren land. This food supply meant that now other living organisms could migrate from the sea. These were *invertebrates*, animals without spinal columns. A scorpion was one of the earliest land pioneers.

At 10:30 P.M. the first of these marine invertebrates began to crawl out of the water. Then came the reptiles, at 10:45. Reptiles became the first animals with spinal columns to be able to live out of water. They were the ancestors of birds, the first of which was archaeopteryx, who showed up roughly 180 million years ago. From 10:45 on, everything was fairly quiet, but just about 11:00 P.M., when many people are thinking about locking up and getting to bed, the dinosaurs arrived.

They lived on (some say ruled) the earth from roughly 11:00 to 11:40, or nearly 150 million years. The dinosaurs were the largest living creatures on earth. Their giant shadows slid across the land as they dominated the planet.

It was definitely a dinosaur's world. Yet within the nooks and crannies of the world scurried smaller life, including the earliest mammals, so called because they produced milk from *mammae*, or breasts. Mammals had to remain small to survive against their huge, already-in-residence neighbors. These small animals could burrow and hide in nature's cubbyholes that were far too tiny for a dinosaur to go poking around in. Small and nocturnal, they lived in the "low rent" district of the dinosaurs' domain.

Then there occurred one of the biggest unsolved mysteries in the history of the earth. At about twenty minutes before midnight, the dinosaurs all disappeared. Not in a single day, not in a year, but perhaps over a few million

NOON TO MIDNIGHT
12:00

11:40 P.M.

RISE OF MAMMALS

NOON TO MIDNIGHT

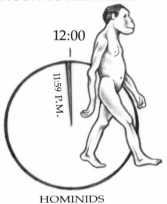

12:00

11:59 P.M.

HOMINIDS

years, which in geological time is quicker than a wink and on our imaginary clock about a minute.

It is thought by some scientists that a large asteroid hit the earth, causing a big cloud of dust to encircle it within a matter of months. Sun could not penetrate the blanketing cloud. There was a long season of darkness. If true, this could have caused the extinction of the dinosaurs as well as other groups of living things. Some survived, such as land plants, crocodiles, and mammals.

In any case, by 11:40 it was all over. The dinosaurs were gone. For millions of years, mammals had failed to make headway against them. Now life in the "low rent" district was over and it was the mammals' turn to dominate the earth, although other life forms continued to develop and change.

The story of the last minute before midnight is an exciting one for us because part of it is ours—the human story. At approximately 11:59 on the imaginary clock, small upright creatures could be seen walking across the open woodlands and plains of Africa and along the shores of ancient lakes. Some walked singly; a few carried infants or led children by the hand. They were perhaps no more than three and a half feet tall. Their heads were small, their brow ridges heavy. Their jaws were slung forward like an ape's. As far as we know, they were the ancestors of all living people today. Our story had begun.

There are scientists who have found a lifetime of work exploring the last minute and fifteen seconds before midnight. These scientists are called *paleoanthropologists*. *Paleontology* is the study of ancient life as revealed in the fossil record. *Fossils* are traces of animals and plants that lived millions of years ago. Sometimes they are prints left in rock or pieces of bones or shells. Paleoanthropologists are specialists who study the fossil remains of our earliest ancestors, members of the human family known as *hominids*. These searchers at the edge of midnight have more questions than answers. Their questions in many instances are the same as many of ours: Who are we? What did our oldest ancestors look like? How have we changed over hundreds of thousands of years? And are we really better and happier than those small upright creatures who walked so long ago?

"You Are Wonderful"

One winter night in 1976, in a laboratory office in the basement of Cleveland's Museum of Natural History, a young scientist stares hard at some rock fragments spread on his desk. A keen observer might recognize a tooth or something like a bone, but most people would think the fragments are nothing more than hunks of rock. They are not. They are fossilized bones over three million years old. The man peers more closely at the bits of teeth and jaw.

What are we? The ancient whispers seem to swirl through the room.

The scientist is Donald Johanson. He is a paleoanthropologist. Two years ago in Ethiopia he discovered the fossils that now lie before him.

This late evening in the laboratory, Johanson is somewhere between hunching and really believing that these fossils are members of the hominid group that led to the evolution of human beings. Hunching, or imagining, is a big part of his job. But he needs to draw facts from his observations, mostly by comparing these fossils with the fossils and bones of humans and apes. Made again and again, these comparisons can show the relationship of this extinct life form to living beings like ourselves.

By comparing and contrasting living organisms, we can visualize a kind of tree with many branches by which living forms grow and interconnect with one another on this earth. We can begin at the top, or most recent, branches and work our way back in time.

Human beings are mammals, and there are other mammals, such as orangutans, gorillas, and chimpanzees, with which we have much in common. Like these animals we have hands that are good at grasping. We have brains that are large compared to our body size. We have forward-facing eyes that enable us to perceive depth and the relative distance between foreground and background. This is called *stereoscopic vision*. We share so much with these animals that together we form a special order of mammals called *primates*. We are related to some more strongly than others—those primates that lack tails, have longer intervals between births, and spend more time with their babies. Along with the great apes—orangutans, chimpanzees, and gorillas—human beings are grouped into a super-family called the hominoidea. Within the hominoidea is a smaller family of creatures who stand erect and walk on two legs. This is the human family, the hominids, and there are only two genera, or kinds: *Australopithecus*, the earliest hominids, now extinct; and *Homo*, human men and women. There used to be more than one species of the genus *Homo*. Now there is only one—our own—*Homo sapiens*, meaning "wise man."

The similarities between ourselves, the australopithecines, and the great apes are inherited from a common ancestor. Features may change over time so that the hand or jawbone of a chimpanzee is not identical to our own. Still, it is possible to understand through certain shared characteristics our historical relationship with living and extinct organisms or species. And this is exactly what paleoanthropologists do as they compare the bones of human beings to those extinct creatures found in the fossil record.

The bones spread out on the table before Don Johanson

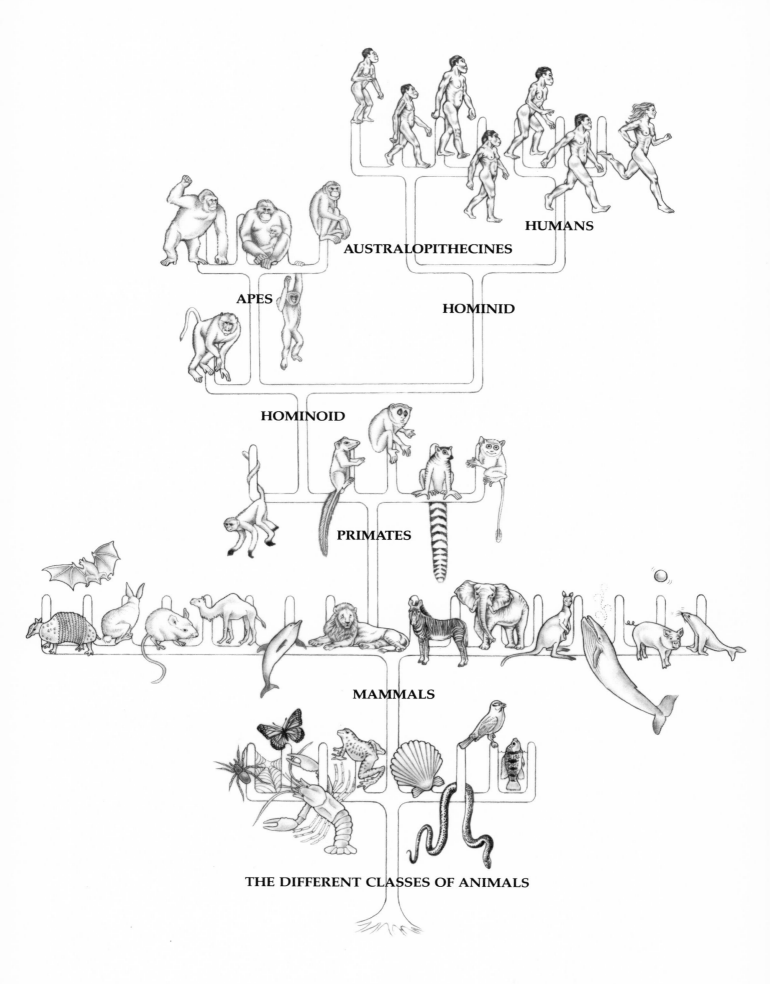

HUMANS

AUSTRALOPITHECINES

APES

HOMINID

HOMINOID

PRIMATES

MAMMALS

THE DIFFERENT CLASSES OF ANIMALS

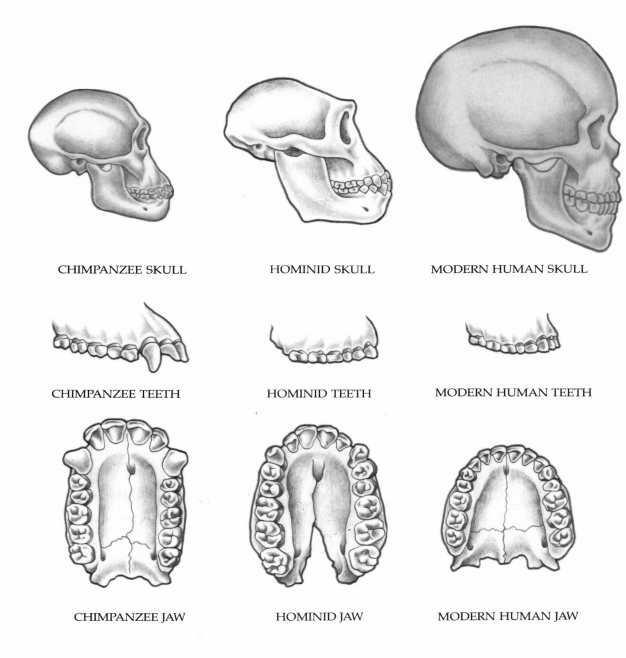

CHIMPANZEE SKULL   HOMINID SKULL   MODERN HUMAN SKULL

CHIMPANZEE TEETH   HOMINID TEETH   MODERN HUMAN TEETH

CHIMPANZEE JAW   HOMINID JAW   MODERN HUMAN JAW

Donald Johanson made comparisons to try to determine what his hominid was.

are definitely hominid, and female—the pelvis tells him that. And her wisdom teeth had been cut, meaning she was a grown-up and not a child. But now Johanson is stuck. The bones of this tiny female, who was barely three feet tall, are like nothing he's seen before. From which twig on the hominid branch had the tiny creature

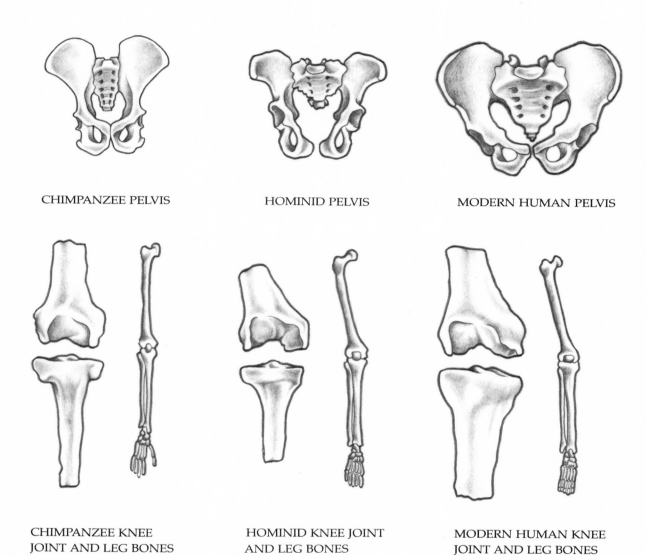

CHIMPANZEE PELVIS

HOMINID PELVIS

MODERN HUMAN PELVIS

CHIMPANZEE KNEE
JOINT AND LEG BONES

HOMINID KNEE JOINT
AND LEG BONES

MODERN HUMAN KNEE
JOINT AND LEG BONES

sprouted? Was she of the genus *Homo* or *Australopithecus*? None of the other australopithecines found prior to 1974 looked quite like her. Could she be a brand-new twig on the hominid limb? The Tree of Life seemed to be growing bushier in front of Johanson's eyes.

It was sheer luck that Johanson ever found this mys-

terious hominid. Five years earlier the fossil bones might still have been buried, waiting to be exposed by wind and rain and the natural forces of erosion. Five years later the bones could have been washed away or crushed. Johanson was excavating in the Afar region of Ethiopia. He had intended to stay in camp and catch up on paperwork, but he had a hunch that day. He wrote in his diary before he left: "Nov. 30, 1974—To locality 162 with Gray in AM. Feel good." He set out with his assistant, Tom Gray, to do some mapping and surveying.

They had been working for a couple of hours and were about to return to camp when Johanson suggested going back by way of a gully. The lucky feeling just wouldn't leave him. The gully proved unpromising and they turned to leave. It was in that instant that Johanson saw a hominid arm. It was so small that Gray thought it must be a monkey's. Johanson shook his head.

"What makes you so sure?" Gray asked.

"That piece next to your hand. That's hominid, too."

Bits of pelvis, ribs, thighbones, skull, and vertebrae seemed to melt out of the dust around them. The two scientists were crouching smack-dab in the middle of a fossil gold mine. It took them a minute to realize what was surrounding them. Then, at just about high noon, two grown-up men could be seen jumping up and down, hugging each other, howling, sweat flying as they danced about like total nuts in the middle of Ethiopia.

They stopped dancing pretty quickly for fear of coming down on a fossil and smashing it. But Johanson and Gray and the other members of the camp were so excited that they never went to bed that night. For the rest of the summer they collected fossil fragments from the gully. Together the pieces made up nearly 40 percent of one single individual. This was special. Never before had such a complete skeleton of one individual hominid that had lived so long ago been found.

One evening Johanson and Gray and their co-workers were listening to taped music. The song that spun out into the Ethiopian night was "Lucy in the Sky with Diamonds," sung by the Beatles. Someone said, "Why don't we call her Lucy?" So she was named. But some call her Denkenesh, an Ethiopian name that means "you are wonderful."

It would be almost three years before they would figure out who Lucy really was.

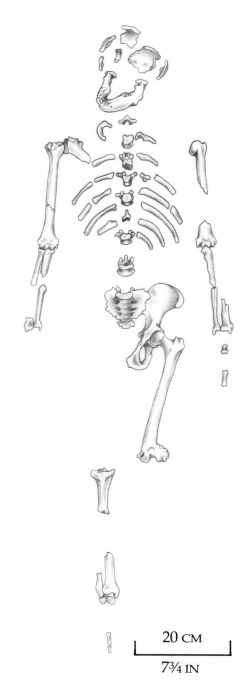

20 CM

7¾ IN

"Lucy" fossil remains

Searchers at the Edge of Midnight

Don Johanson and many of his associates had traveled a long way to search for the being they named Lucy. They had come to a part of eastern Africa they knew was particularly rich in fossil bones.

When paleoanthropologists suspect that a region might be rich in fossils, they examine the ground for clues that there may be something worth digging for beneath the earth. A few test trenches may be dug. If bones or stone tools and other promising finds are discovered, most likely the area will be declared a "site."

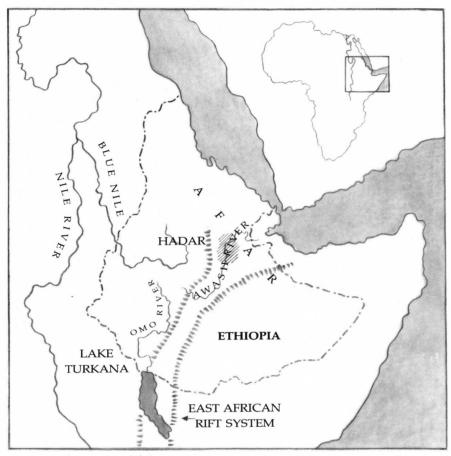

Fossil-rich eastern Africa

Once a site is established, hundreds of thousands of dollars from foundations, governments, and universities are sought to support a team of scientists and workers to excavate the site and evaluate the finds.

An excavation team is made up of a number of people with different specialties. Often there are also students who are not yet specialists but who have a deep interest in the work.

A typical team excavating hominid fossil remains would consist of a geologist, an archaeologist, a paleontologist, a paleoanthropologist, surveyors, excavators, mapmakers, scientific illustrators, and people trained in the fine art of fossil reconstruction.

21

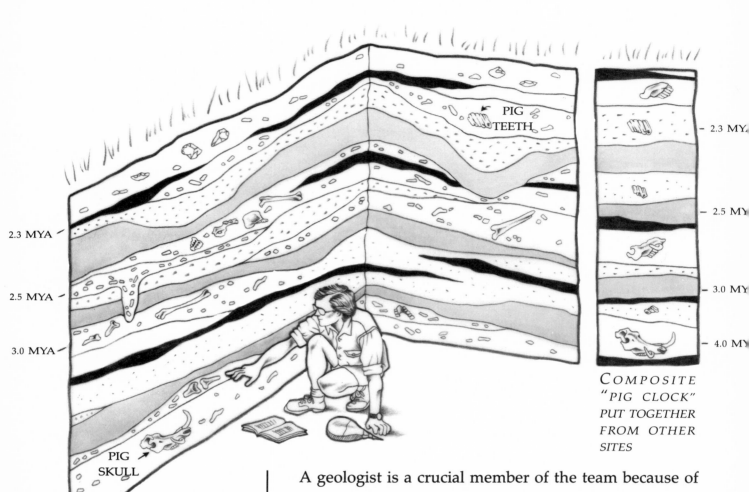

2.3 MYA

2.5 MYA

3.0 MYA

4.0 MYA

PIG
TEETH

PIG
SKULL

*COMPOSITE
"PIG CLOCK"
PUT TOGETHER
FROM OTHER
SITES*

— 2.3 MY

— 2.5 MY

— 3.0 MY

— 4.0 MY

A geologist is a crucial member of the team because of his knowledge of the earth's crust. He can read the layers, or strata, of soil, rock, and sand and other materials and reconstruct the sequence in time when the different layers were laid down. This sequence, called the *stratigraphy*, helps the other scientists interpret what happened and in what order. Stratigraphy is crucial to figuring out a site's age and the manner in which stones and bones have been preserved. The strata are built of sedimentary rock, deposited layer by layer. What is on top is the most recent, the youngest. What is below and deeper is older.

In eastern Africa a key to the stratigraphic time frame turned out to be pigs. Paleontologist Basil Cooke was an expert on extinct pigs, and he had been called in to help the geologists determine more closely the ages of the various strata. Millions of years before, many different kinds of pigs had lived in Africa. Cooke had traced these pigs over a two-million-year period, and he knew when each kind of pig had lived. Because different kinds of pigs lived at different times, the bony remains of the pigs could be used as a "pig clock" to crosscheck and sometimes narrow the time range of the strata.

Archaeologists look through the "trash" of the past, the material traces left by human activity. From this evidence they try to understand early life. The farther back an archaeologist travels in time, the dimmer the impression left by people on the earth. There was a time when there was no art and no tools and the earth's people slept in the open or perhaps in trees and, much later, in simple huts. The archaeological record preserves mainly stone, bone, and, from later periods, pottery; and most of the signs of earliest human activity vanished soon after they appeared. But from what has been left at a site, archaeologists try to uncover patterns of human activity.

As we've seen, a paleontologist is a specialist in fossil evidence, and paleoanthropologists like Don Johanson are in search of our earliest ancestors. The surveyors are men and women who usually have very keen eyesight, a good knowledge of the terrain, and an almost magical ability to detect fossil clues on the surface of the land that other people might quickly pass by. Hominid fossils, after all, do not call attention to themselves—"Hey, look at me!" The terrain in these regions is often rough and scrabbly. A fossil fragment on the surface can look like a clod of dirt or chunk of rock. Many of the surveyors, as might be

expected, live in the region in which an excavation is conducted. Johanson found the Afar people of Ethiopia very valuable to his work there.

Most of the team members who are specialists have had experience and training in excavation. Students who are not yet specialists are immediately trained in the fine and often hot and monotonous work of digging. They do not dig with big shovels, as one might imagine. Excavators use a variety of small tools, ranging from trowels to dental picks, whisk brooms, small paintbrushes, and dustpans, to carefully brush or scrape away the layers of the earth. Nothing is thrown away unexamined. Before it is discarded even the soil is passed through a sieve to isolate the smallest fragments of stone or bone.

Before the digging begins, a map, called the *site plan*, is made of the site. This map divides the area to be excavated into units. Each unit is marked by stakes, string, or tape, and every single piece of material excavated from a unit is carefully recorded in a site notebook as to its precise location in the stratigraphy. Later it will be sketched, measured, and photographed.

Near the site, often within walking distance, is the camp, the living quarters for the team of people who work at the site. Very few archaeological sites are near cities, or even small towns. Most often the best sites are found in remote places, far from cities or towns. Everything from food to shelter must be trucked in and the camp itself must be built. For the most part these camps are temporary, for use during the digging season, so there are tents instead of buildings and cots with sleeping bags instead of beds with sheets. There is no plumbing for toilets, so latrines must be dug. Water for drinking is often scarce, so it must be brought in in barrels. Water for bathing might

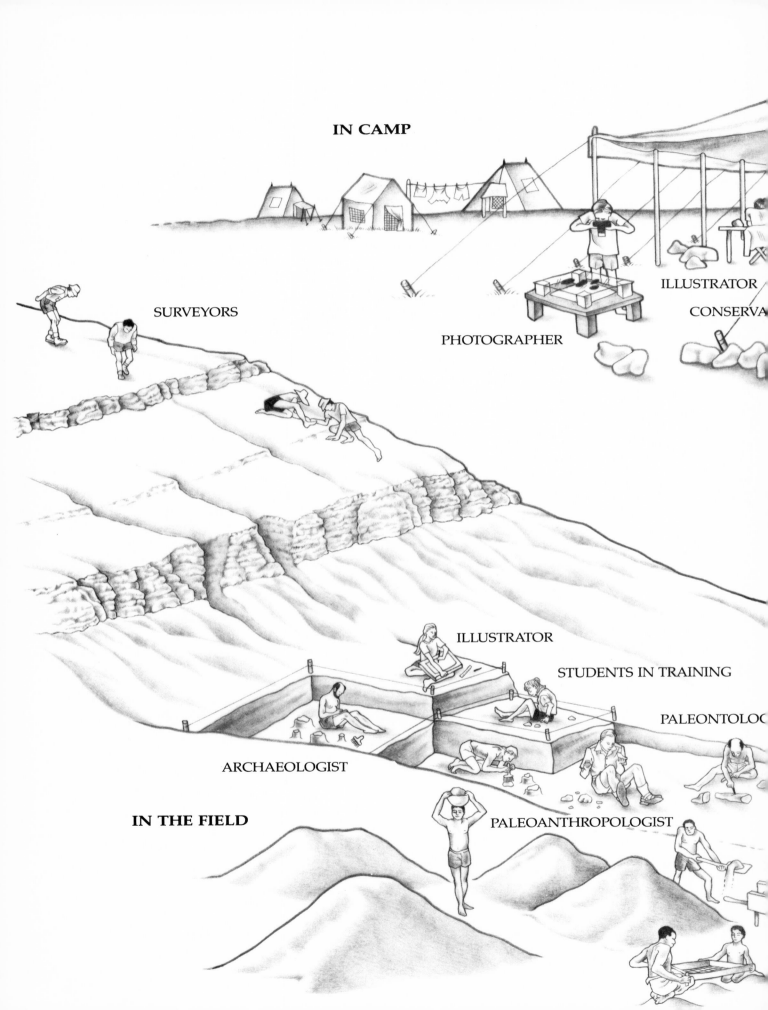

IN CAMP

SURVEYORS

PHOTOGRAPHER

ILLUSTRATOR

CONSERVA

ILLUSTRATOR

STUDENTS IN TRAINING

PALEONTOLO

ARCHAEOLOGIST

IN THE FIELD

PALEOANTHROPOLOGIST

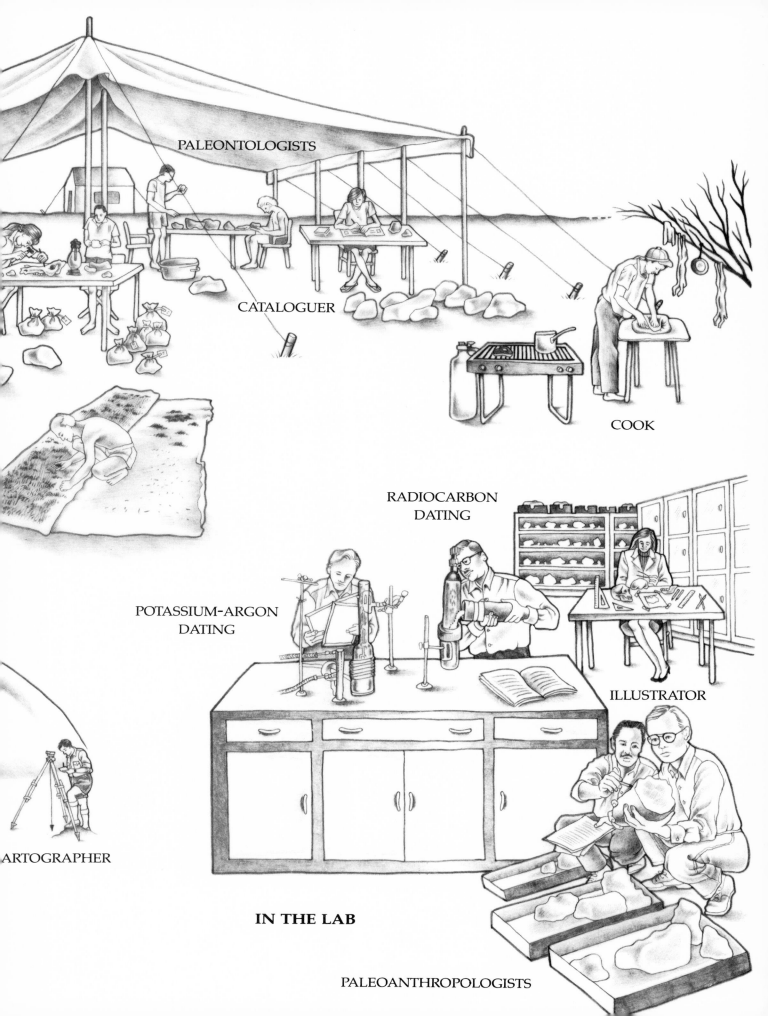

PALEONTOLOGISTS

CATALOGUER

COOK

RADIOCARBON
DATING

POTASSIUM-ARGON
DATING

ILLUSTRATOR

ARTOGRAPHER

IN THE LAB

PALEOANTHROPOLOGISTS

be available from nearby lakes. In Africa, however, many of these lakes have large, people-eating crocodiles, so workers bathe with extreme caution.

One of the most important workers in a camp is the cook. He or she must be skilled in preparing three meals a day with perhaps nothing more than an outdoor grill and an ice chest. If there was enough money, a butane-powered stove and refrigerator may have been purchased. Still, the nearest grocery may be hundreds of miles away, so if the meals are poorly planned the team can get cranky, and if the team gets cranky the work will not go well, and if the work gets sloppy the site will get a bad reputation, and if that happens no more money will come in to fund the excavation!

The field laboratory is usually housed in a tent. Artifacts, fossils, pollen samples, soil samples, and all the materials that have been excavated and recorded in the field are sorted, analyzed, evaluated, and stored. If the fragments of a skull have been found, it is here that people skilled in reconstruction begin to try to piece the human jigsaw puzzle together. Detailed drawings by trained archaeo-logical illustrators are done. All the materials are carefully catalogued and recorded and studied in the lab tent. At the end of the season they will be packed up and taken back to universities for even closer study—in particular, for more accurate dating.

Stratigraphy can give the relative age of an object—whether it is older or younger than some other object from another layer. But an absolute date, in which the number of years ago can be estimated, requires procedures that are more complicated and cannot be done in the field labs. Radiocarbon dating and potassium-argon dating are two methods used for figuring dates more precisely. Radiocarbon dating measures the amount of radioactive carbon that has survived in fossils less than fifty thousand years old. Potassium-argon dating measures the rate at which potassium decays into argon (a gaseous element) in volcanic material found near fossils. It has been used to date fossils millions of years old.

To determine the age of Lucy, Johanson used plain stratigraphical analysis and potassium-argon dating, as well as the evidence provided by Basil Cooke's pig clock. These three methods were used to cross-check and confirm and finally determine that Lucy had lived and walked upright over three million years ago.

The Man Who Saw Things Differently

Sir Charles Lyell

In the early nineteenth century the science of geology was new. In 1830 Charles Lyell, a brilliant scientist, published *Principles of Geology*, which introduced an idea we find commonplace today: the idea of *geological change*. He believed that the earth was always changing and that by studying everyday geological events, such as erosion by wind and water, earthquakes, and volcanic eruptions, great changes such as the creation of mountain ranges could be explained, as well as such contradictions as the discovery of ocean or deep-sea fossils on mountaintops.

What Lyell's understanding of geology provided was time—"deep time," enough time for oceans to disappear and for mountains to form from materials once on the sea-floor. Fossils were being discovered in the different strata of the earth, and early paleontologists, aided by the work of geologists such as Charles Lyell, began to form a picture of a very, very ancient world, an earth in which there was enough time for living things to change, or evolve.

This picture was not one that many people were happy to see. Calculations based on events in the Old Testament led people to believe that the earth was only 6,000 years old; they thought fossils were the result of a number of catastrophic floods in which God destroyed all life on earth and then restocked it with brand-new species. To admit that the earth had changed naturally over a vast period of time would have meant violating their most basic beliefs.

These people clung to their faith that all things, living and nonliving, were arranged in a rigid order. This order was sometimes called the Great Chain of Being. God was at the very top. Just beneath God were other divine beings, such as angels; then came the stars and then the elements, which were air and fire, water and earth. Then came man, the link in the chain between heaven and earth. Next were the animals, the plants, and finally the metals of the earth. Everything had its place and, most important, it was supposed to stay there.

"Vast chain of Being! which from God began, / Natures ethereal, human, angel, man, / Beast, bird, fish, insect . . ." So wrote Alexander Pope in the eighteenth century. He, like a lot of other people, imagined himself linked to all the earth's creatures in a spiritual order. And when he considered his own position in the chain he looked up and not down:

Charles Darwin in 1840

"Men would be angels, Angels would be Gods, / Why has not man a microscopic eye?. . .For this plain reason, man is not a fly. / Say what the use were finer optics given, T'inspect a mite, not comprehend the heaven."

Charles Darwin saw the world just a little bit differently. He was born in 1809. He was not a terrific student. It has been said that by today's standards he could not have made it into college. He liked hunting, shooting, gambling, and beetles. He was very fond of beetles and had gathered an impressive collection. He loved natural history in general. He studied medicine at Edinburgh College but couldn't stand the sight of blood, so he switched to Cambridge University to study for the clergy. There he was forced to take courses in the classics, which he hated, and mathematics, which confused him. He took comfort in belonging to the Glutton Club, but his favorite activities were mucking about in the countryside and boating down rivers collecting beetles, butterflies, and different kinds of flowers. Unfortunately, chasing about with a butterfly net was considered a hobby and not a profession for a young gentleman of that time.

It had been planned by Charles's father that when Charles finished his theological studies at Cambridge he would become a vicar in a country church. And when Charles graduated in 1831, he thought that was exactly what he would do.

He barely made it through his last exam, but like a lot of young people whose lives are carefully arranged by grown-ups, everything did not go exactly according to plan. The August after he graduated from Cambridge, a friend who shared Charles's passion for natural history arranged a position for him as ship's naturalist on a surveying vessel called the HMS *Beagle*. On September 5 Charles was summoned to England to meet the *Beagle*'s captain, Robert FitzRoy. The *Beagle* was a square-rigged ship about to set sail on a two-year voyage around the world. Its purpose was to survey coastal waters and islands and to sail as far as possible toward the frozen south. Darwin would spend his time observing, collecting, and studying specimens of life all over the world, but particularly in South America.

His father had a fit. His family tried to dissuade him. They warned him of seasickness and predicted that gallivanting about collecting bugs would ruin his prospects of being a clergyman. But finally his father reluctantly gave his consent.

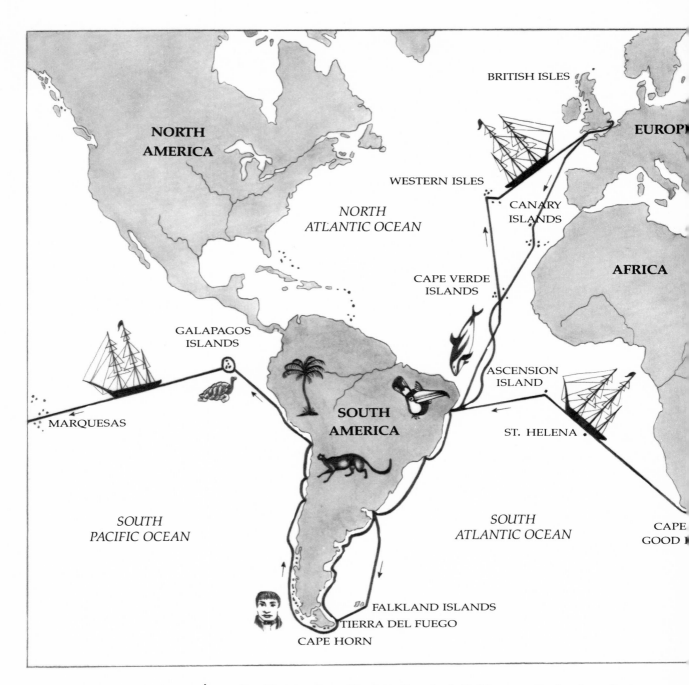

On December 10 the *Beagle* left Plymouth harbor but was driven back in by adverse winds. On December 21 they tried again and were once more slammed back into port. Darwin, as predicted, was violently seasick. Finally on December 27 the wind turned fair and the *Beagle* set out on a voyage that would alter people's view of themselves and their earth forever.

In the year 1831, no prehistoric human fossil remains

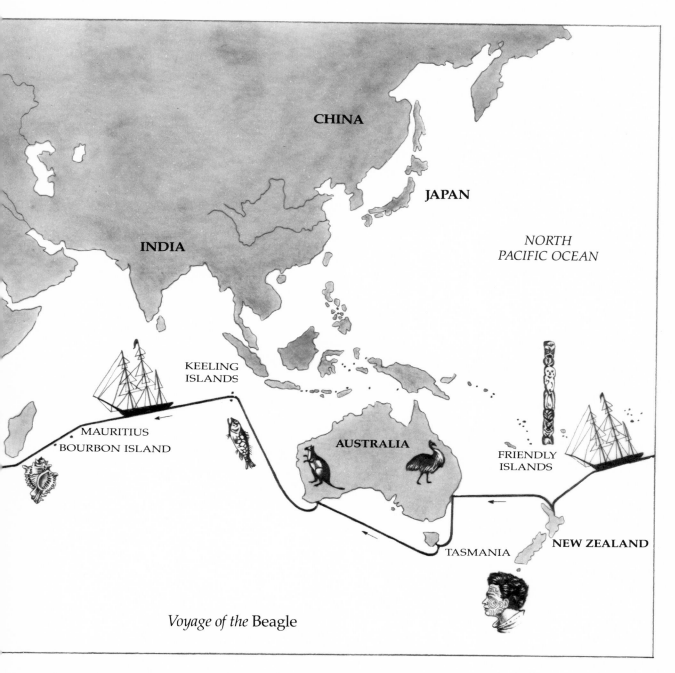

Voyage of the Beagle

had yet been unearthed. People knew that certain characteristics or traits could be inherited and passed on. But they believed that the basic human form remained unchanged, just as they believed that everyone should know his or her place in society and stay there.

But Darwin observed with increasing fascination the relationships between living things separated by geography—animals and plants of the islands off the coast of

Among the individual members of every population of plants and animals, there are hereditary differences.

Some of these hereditary traits give individuals a better chance to survive and reproduce.

South America and those of the mainland—and between those separated in time—living things and recently extinct forms that were related but not identical. These observations led him to suspect that living things changed over great periods of time. On reading Charles Lyell, Darwin realized how very ancient the earth was and that in fact there was enough time for Lyell's theories to be true. He did not write his classic work, *Origin of Species*, on the voyage. He merely began to observe that life was a series of connected changes over long periods of time, making it possible for one form to develop into another.

Consequently, these traits become more prevalent in later generations.

The voyage of the *Beagle* lasted for five years, not two, and Darwin would not publish his theories for over another twenty years. He knew perfectly well how people would react to his ideas: the notion that life forms were not fixed but always changing, and that living things were the result not of separate creations but of long, intertwining biological histories. People who believed in a Divine Plan would greet with scant enthusiasm his theory of natural selection, which proposed that as conditions in nature changed so did living forms and that those animals with traits best suited for new conditions survived.

A cartoon of Charles Darwin as a monkey that appeared at the time of the publication of Origin of Species.

Before Darwin there was no need to ask where we came from. People had always been people, bugs were bugs, and birds had always been birds. But Darwin turned all that inside out, and for the first time it was possible to discuss the origins of animals and plants.

Darwin, a shy man, was reluctant to stir up controversy. In 1858 a young naturalist named Alfred Russel Wallace, totally independently of Darwin, developed the theory of natural selection. Darwin was finally forced to write his book on evolution because Wallace was about to beat him to the punch.

One thousand two hundred fifty copies of *Origin of Species* were published. They sold out in a single day. And although Darwin believed most firmly that human beings, too, had descended from an earlier form, he was careful not to mention man. He believed this would be too much for people to accept and might prejudice some against the general ideas in the book.

With Darwin, the Great Chain of Being finally came apart, and in its place a kind of Tree of Life was sprouting with intertwining limbs and branches. But Darwin did not think that his theories were at odds with a belief in God. In the final paragraph of *Origin of Species* he wrote, "There is a grandeur in this view of life, with its several powers, having been originally breathed by the creator into a few forms or into one . . . from so simple a beginning endless forms most beautiful and most wonderful have been and are being evolved."

Later he wrote, "In each great region of the world the living mammals are closely related to the extinct species of the same region. It is therefore probable that Africa was formerly inhabited by extinct apes closely allied to the gorilla and chimpanzee; and as these two species are now man's nearest allies, it is somewhat more than probable that our early progenitors lived on the African continent than elsewhere."

It was a good hunch, and it sent Don Johanson and countless other paleoanthropologists of this century to Africa.

A Road Divides

If on our imaginary clock Lucy arrived at 11:59, who was there in the seconds before her? That was when a kind of branching occurred in the Tree of Life, during the epoch known as the Miocene, which began twenty-six million years ago.

Branching means that some members within a group separate from others. It is as if a fork in the road has been reached and some follow one way and the others, another. The diverging branches live and breed apart, in areas geo-graphically isolated from one another. Before they reach

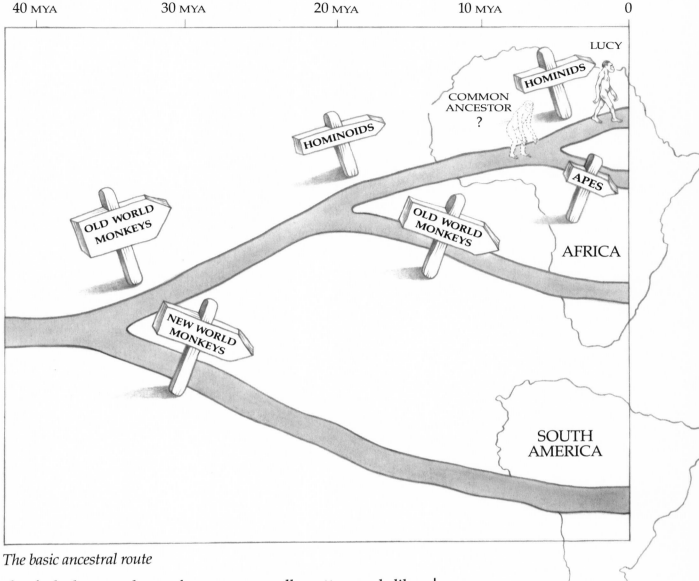

LUCY

HOMINIDS

COMMON ANCESTOR ?

HOMINOIDS

APES

OLD WORLD MONKEYS

OLD WORLD MONKEYS

AFRICA

NEW WORLD MONKEYS

SOUTH AMERICA

The basic ancestral route

the fork the members of a group are all pretty much like each other, but after the fork they begin to change and develop differently. Sometimes they change in small ways, sometimes in big ways.

Charles Darwin did not actually watch this process going on, of course. But when he was in South America he could see that many species, while separated geographically, were still similar to one another in various ways. From these and other observations he made a very good guess that these species evolved from some common

41

ancestor. Since Darwin's time, repeated observations of species have shown that his logic was right.

Ten million years before the Miocene all the monkeys that existed looked very much alike. Then they, too, reached a fork. One group remained in Africa. The others migrated to South America and became known as New World Monkeys, for that is where they diversified, or became different—the New World, South America. Those that stayed where they were came to be called Old World Monkeys. It is from the ancestors of today's Old World Monkeys that the road leading to apes and humans branched.

Chimpanzees that we see in zoos or in documentary movies on television are not our ancient ancestors, but chimpanzees and humans have descended from a common ancestor. We know this because we share with these modern apes many features—among them forward-facing eyes and grasping hands with nails, not claws. Humans and apes are connected with this common ancestor by separate links.

Our common ancestor stood at a second big fork in the road. The apes took one branch, hominids another. Who stood at this fork? Who was our last common ancestor, the one we shared with the apes?

There have been many contenders for the title. Lucy, a hominid, stands closest to the fork for now. But scientists have been looking for a much older creature, and they can approach the fork from the near side or the far side.

Paleoanthropologists interested in the near side of the fork trace back through the hominid line hoping to reach, at the very beginning, our common ancestor with the apes. Donald Johanson is a paleoanthropologist who explores the near side of the fork.

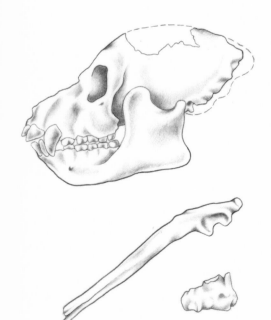

Aegyptopithecus *fossils— Dawn Ape*

Other paleoanthropologists search on the far side of the fork, in the ancient time when there weren't any hominids at all. These men and women are especially interested in finding fossils of extinct apes. They study the fossilized bones they find and compare them to other extinct apes as well as to living ones in order to better place these creatures on the Tree of Life and to figure out which branches might lead to a last common ancestor.

The far side of the fork is a hard terrain to explore. It is the time of the long-vanished apes of the Miocene. And the fossils of these apes are very rare and difficult to understand. One of the very earliest of these creatures was *Aegyptopithecus*. It is also called the Dawn Ape, for it is over thirty million years old. It was discovered by paleoanthropologist Elwyn Simons. Simons felt that this animal, which had thirty-two teeth, as humans do, might be the oldest direct ancestor of humans yet found.

There are few things harder to find than a direct ancestral route. Not every living form is able to change with its environment. Those that can't become extinct. The fossil record is filled with extinct species, and sometimes the differences between fossils of extinct and living species are very small. It's up to paleontologists to figure out which ancestors are on the branches leading to a modern species, such as ourselves, and which are on the side branches, extinct.

Any scientist would feel very special if he or she discovered one of our ancient ancestors. So scientists who scour the fossil record on the far side of the fork most often go to Africa, where the great apes still live. There they hope to find the fossils of an extinct species that was closely related to the chimpanzees or gorillas of today. Perhaps it was one of these extinct apes that stood at the fork, the common ancestor to both humans and apes.

After the Dawn Ape a few other fossil apes of the Miocene were found that could possibly have been ancestors to modern apes. One was called *Proconsul*, named after a famous chimpanzee who lived in the London Zoo. However, at one point in the fossil record it seems as if the road just dips into a bottomless pit. Between eight and four million years ago the fossil record yields almost nothing. Before this "hole," the fossil record reveals that there were very ancient Miocene apes, like *Aegyptopithecus*, scampering about on all fours or swinging through trees. And then—nothing. We can imagine a small ancient ape tumbling into the hole eight million years ago and popping out four million years later upright, walking, and ready for life as a hominid, but still with an apelike face and brain. A finishing school for apes keen on becoming human! But the hole is simply a hole, a gap in the fossil record. Everything that we have learned so far about the origins of life is due to flukes, fortunate accidents that occur when the processes of erosion literally pull back the earth's crust and reveal a few scraps of our history. There is a huge amount of information that cannot be reached until the mechanisms of geology and the whims of nature expose a little bit more. The paleoanthropologist has to be lucky.

Sometimes a paleoanthropologist need not go all the way to Africa to make an important find. Elwyn Simons made a startling discovery as he "excavated" an old file drawer in the laboratory of Yale University's Peabody Museum of Natural History. The Peabody Museum had long been a distinguished supporter of paleontological explorations. It was founded by O. C. Marsh, a nineteenth-century scientist who was responsible for digging up some

Reconstruction of Dryopithecus—Proconsul. *The shaded areas show the bones actually found.*

44

Elwyn Simons at the Peabody Museum

of the first dinosaur bones discovered in North America. The museum and its laboratories were a treasure trove of fossils belonging to the most ancient creatures that had ever squirmed, crawled, hopped, lumbered, or walked upright across the face of the earth. Elwyn Simons merely pulled open a file drawer and saw two fragments from a single upper jawbone and a few teeth. The pieces had been excavated in northern India and Pakistan in the 1930s by another paleoanthropologist, who had declared them to belong to a creature he called Rama Ape, or *Ramapithecus*. Rama was the name of a mythical Hindu prince. After an initial flurry of interest the fossil pieces were put away and forgotten for nearly thirty years, until Simons opened the drawer.

Although there were only a few small pieces of fossil, certain humanlike characteristics caught Simons's eye. It was as if hundreds of very big questions tumbled out of the file drawer, too. Who was this creature? Where did it

45

David Pilbeam

belong in the Tree of Life? If it were indeed the ancestor at the fork in the road, when had the fork occurred? Joining Simons in his research was another scientist from England, David Pilbeam. Together they began trying to piece together one of the great picture puzzles of evolutionary history.

David Pilbeam's family had hoped that he would become an engineer, but he had no interest in engineering. For a while he studied medicine at Cambridge University in England but found that he had more questions about the history of life on earth than could ever be answered by becoming a medical doctor. So he decided to study paleoanthropology. With his insatiable appetite for what, when, and how questions, David Pilbeam could not have chosen a better career.

Ramapithecus was similar to many of the apes on the far side of the fork, and yet it was intriguingly different. *Could it have been our last common ancestor?* Simons and Pilbeam thought there was a good chance. Although most of the palate and the front part of the jaw were missing, there were features in these jaw fragments that were similar to human features—especially the small size of the canine teeth. And both Simons and Pilbeam imagined that these humanlike teeth probably formed a rounded dental arcade, the curved bony structure beneath the gums from which teeth grow. In apes the dental arcade is shaped more like a box.

The two men also felt that this creature most likely had walked upright and perhaps had even used tools for hunting and preparing food. They suspected this because *Ramapithecus*'s teeth seemed so similar to our own—far too small for tearing flesh from prey as animals might do. Instead of strong teeth and incisors, perhaps *Ramapithecus*

46

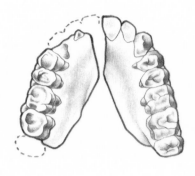

THE UPPER JAW FRAGMENTS OF *RAMAPITHECUS*, AS RECONSTRUCTED BY ELWYN SIMONS

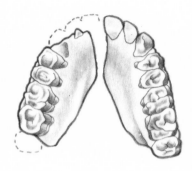 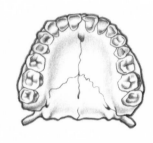 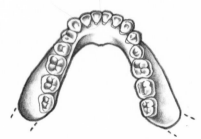

SIMONS'S RECONSTRUCTION COMPARED TO THE ROUNDED HUMAN UPPER AND LOWER JAWS

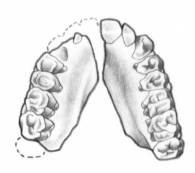 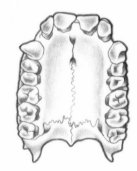 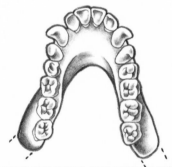

SIMONS'S RECONSTRUCTION COMPARED TO THE MORE RECTANGULAR CHIMPANZEE UPPER AND LOWER JAWS

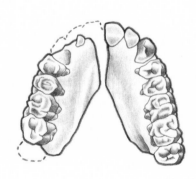 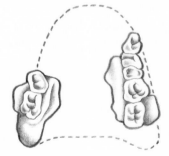 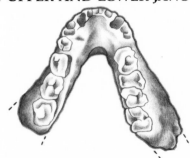

NEW FINDS FROM PAKISTAN OF UPPER AND LOWER JAWS OF *RAMAPITHECUS* HAD A MORE BOXLIKE SHAPE, CLOSER TO APE THAN HUMAN.

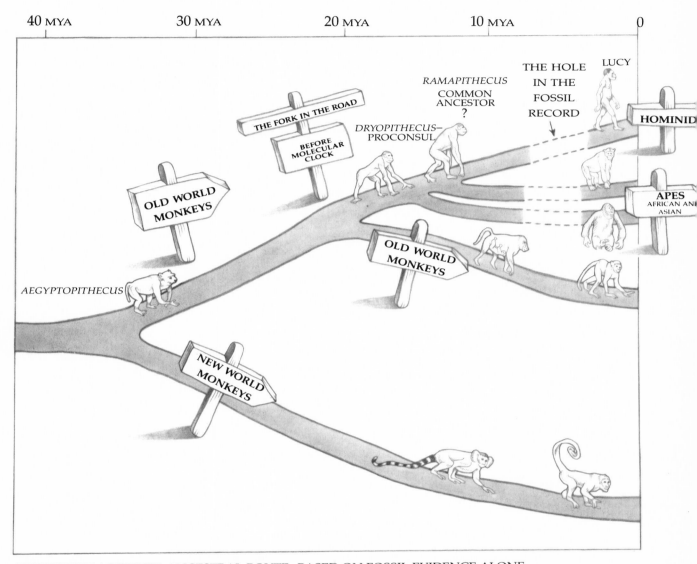

PREVIOUSLY ACCEPTED ANCESTRAL ROUTE, BASED ON FOSSIL EVIDENCE ALONE

had other "tools." If *Ramapithecus* had walked upright, then its hands would have been free to hold tools. It all fit.

Based on a few fragmentary pieces from a jawbone, Simons and Pilbeam had constructed a walking, tool-using creature who stood obligingly at the fork in the road. But as in any scientific inquiry new pieces of information continued to be found.

More *Ramapithecus* fossils were excavated in Pakistan—

48

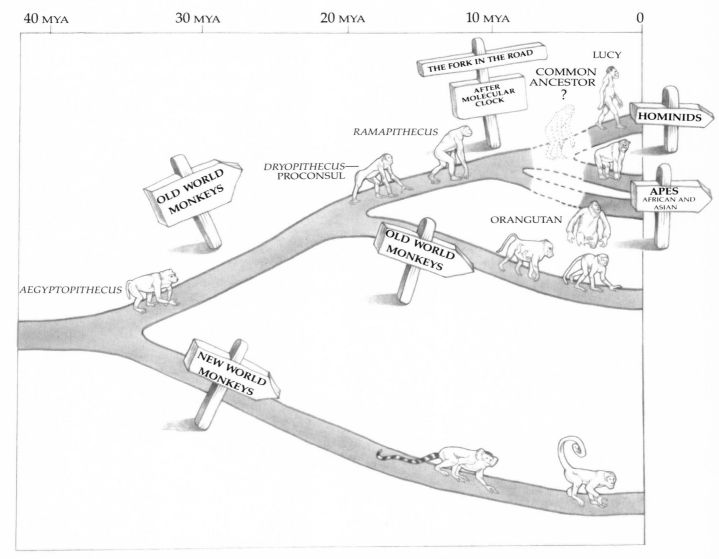

Timeline labels: 40 MYA, 30 MYA, 20 MYA, 10 MYA, 0

THE FORK IN THE ROAD
AFTER MOLECULAR CLOCK
LUCY
COMMON ANCESTOR ?
HOMINIDS
RAMAPITHECUS
OLD WORLD MONKEYS
DRYOPITHECUS—PROCONSUL
ORANGUTAN
OLD WORLD MONKEYS
APES
AFRICAN AND ASIAN
AEGYPTOPITHECUS
NEW WORLD MONKEYS

CURRENTLY ACCEPTED ANCESTRAL ROUTE, BASED ON FOSSIL AND "MOLECULAR CLOCK" EVIDENCE

and more fragments from the jaw. The rounded dental arcade so characteristic of humans began to fade in front of David Pilbeam's eyes as he held the new evidence and saw its boxlike dental arcade.

New biochemical studies were proving that molecules can tell as much, if not more, about the relationship between humans and apes as fossils can. Blood contains proteins. The chemistry of those proteins can be compared between living species. The more closely related two species are, the more similar their blood proteins are expected to be. And so the greater the difference between blood proteins, the longer ago those two species had forked apart.

Our blood proteins are very nearly identical to those of chimpanzees, and it was calculated on what has been called the *molecular clock* that humans and apes had separated from each other about five million years ago. *Ramapithecus* simply could not have been at that fork. It had been firmly dated as having lived as many as fourteen million years ago. And finally it was discovered that *Ramapithecus* was related to orangutans, which split off within the hominoidea several millions of years before gorillas and chimpanzees and the line that eventually produced human beings.

It would take Elwyn Simons a bit longer to accept the new facts about *Ramapithecus* than it did David Pilbeam. But just because Pilbeam conceded earlier did not make him any happier at being wrong.

He had studied and hunched and hoped that *Ramapithecus* was the ancestor at the fork in the road. The new evidence disproved that, and the little ape prince that might have been human was toppled from his throne. How did Pilbeam feel?

"I will never again cling so firmly to one particular evolutionary scheme," Pilbeam wrote in 1978. "And I have come to believe that many statements we make about the hows and whys of human evolution say as much about us . . . as about anything that 'really' happened."

Pilbeam and Simons expected, as did many others, to find that the earliest hominid was a pretty special creature. With such notions it was all too easy to see in *Ramapithecus* what they wanted to find. When new information came in, Pilbeam, although disappointed, was excited, too. "Many things ran through my mind," he reported, "feelings of exhilaration and happiness for the expedition, for the discoverers [of the new fossils from Pakistan], satisfaction for myself; but more than anything my mind was beginning to think along new lines, because I could see our previous beliefs about *Ramapithecus* and the whole story of human origins needed re-thinking."

Footprints in the Ashes

In the language of the Masai tribespeople of Tanzania, *laetoli* means "red lily," a flower which grows there in profusion and from which the Laetoli region of Tanzania, in East Africa, takes its name. In Laetoli, about 3.6 million years ago, an important story was inscribed in layers of volcanic ash. It is a story from the near side of the fork—a story written not in bones, but in prints, hominid footprints.

The prints were discovered in 1976 by paleoanthropologist Mary Leakey and her archaeological team. Nearly forty years before, Mary had visited Laetoli with her husband, Louis, another great fossil expert, who died in 1972. At that time they were not convinced that there was enough there to dig for. Mary Leakey continued to feel mysteriously drawn to Laetoli, as if something had eluded them in the beds of rich volcanic ash. In 1975 she began to assemble a team of excavators and directed their efforts to the Laetoli strata that had been firmly dated as being at least 2.4 million years old. A year later the footprints were found.

Mary Leakey has scrutinized, measured, and wondered about these prints since that day in 1976.

The footprints point north. Originally, they were thought to have belonged to two individuals, walking together but not side by side. One might have been male; the other, female. The prints go for seventy-seven feet and end suddenly where streams have eroded the fossil record. But at one point along the seventy-seven-foot trail, one of the walkers stopped, paused, and turned to the left, possibly to glance at some threat or irregularity. "This motion," wrote Mary Leakey, "so intensely human, transcends time. Three million six hundred thousand years ago, a remote ancestor—just as you or I—experienced a moment of doubt."

As the footprints were studied, scientists made an astonishing discovery. One set is in fact *two* sets of feet. A third, smaller hominid had walked in the prints left by one of the larger individuals in much the same manner that children today often "try on" their parents' footprints as they walk on the wet, packed sand of a beach in the summertime. We can imagine that this double set of prints shows playing and imitating; as such, it seems very human.

53

There is a single characteristic that distinguishes all hominids from apes and other primates: the ability to walk erect, or bipedally. Mary Leakey's excavations in the Laetoli volcanic beds gave the world the first absolute proof that hominids had walked erect over three million years ago. This was not long—in evolutionary terms—after the fork in the road where apes and hominids separated.

Now that scientists know when hominids walked upright, one of the liveliest topics of debate is why they stood up in the first place. Nobody knows for sure but almost everybody has an idea. This is one question that fires the imaginations of anthropologists, paleoanthropologists, and archaeologists alike.

They stood up to see over the grass, some scientists say. About five or six million years ago there was a major change in the climate of the earth. In Africa the air became cooler and drier. Forests retreated and grasslands, the savannah, expanded. There were not as many trees to climb. Maybe the apelike creatures of that continent *did* want to see what was over the grass. The savannah would become their new habitat, and those creatures who walked erect could better adapt to the new opportunities of this changing environment.

Standing up freed the hands to carry. Some people feel that hominids stood up to carry weapons. Others believe that hominids stood up to carry tools—tools to help them find and carry food, such as digging sticks and crude containers. This is all speculation, because wood tools or grass baskets would not remain in the fossil record and there is no evidence that harder materials were used by hominids as far back as 3.75 million years ago.

Although the Laetoli hominids trekked through the wet

The Laetoli footprints with workers

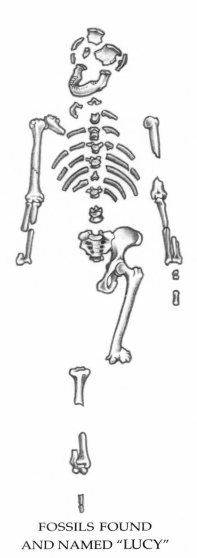

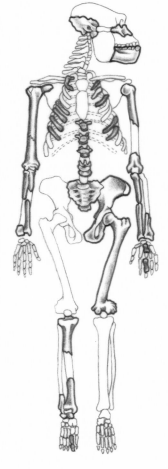

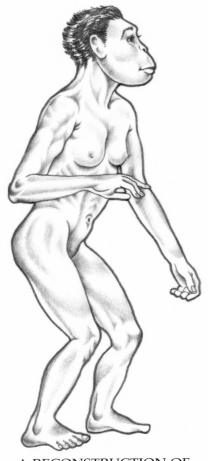

FOSSILS FOUND
AND NAMED "LUCY"

RECONSTRUCTION INTO
A FULL SKELETON

A RECONSTRUCTION OF
AUSTRALOPITHECUS AFARENSIS
USING THE "LUCY" SKELETON AND
OTHER HADAR FOSSILS

volcanic ash a little before the time of Lucy, it is possible that they were related to the tiny hominid woman found in the Afar badlands of Ethiopia. But where in the Tree of Life did they all belong?

Don Johanson discovered Lucy in 1974. In 1976, when Mary Leakey was excavating the Laetoli footprints, Johanson and his teamworkers discovered the bones of at least thirteen individuals who had died at the same time.

56

They became known as the First Family. All of these hominids seemed to be crying out for identification, and Johanson and his colleague Tim White were stumped.

Johanson was convinced Lucy was not human. She was just too little and her brain was too small. Her jaw seemed curved, closer to a human being's but still protruding like an ape's. Johanson decided it would be helpful to examine the casts of the Laetoli prints along with some fossil jaw fragments and teeth from the same region. He was struck by certain similarities between these fossils and those of Lucy and the First Family.

Johanson and Tim White began an analysis of all the fossil fragments. They made lists and endless comparisons between these early hominids and the fossil remains of hominids who lived later. They concluded that these hominids from Afar and Laetoli stood halfway between the great apes and man. And they were unique enough to require a brand-new name.

They were definitely not human, so they would not be categorized as *Homo*. Johanson placed Lucy and the First Family and the Laetoli fossils in the genus *Australopithecus* and named the species *Australopithecus afarensis*, or "southern ape of the Afar region."

This made Mary Leakey very angry. First, she believed that her fossils were *Homo*, "true man," or at least in the direct line of human beings. Second, she did not like the idea that her fossils from Laetoli, Tanzania, had been used to define a species that was named after a region in Ethiopia. She felt that her discoveries had been arbitrarily lumped in with the others and given a name that had little to do with what they really were or where they had come from.

Mary Leakey and Don Johanson were not simply ar-

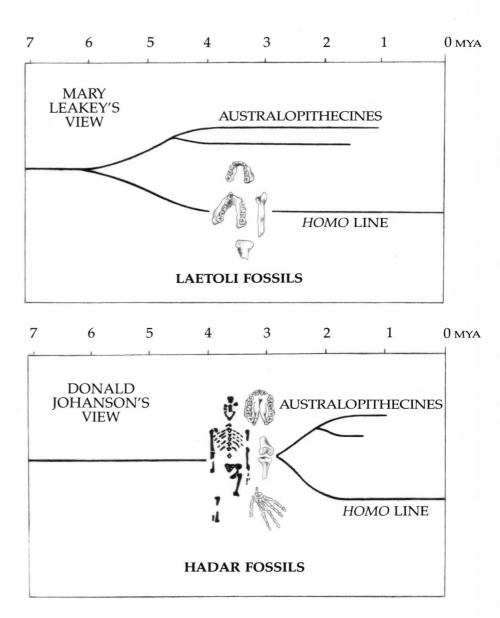

7 6 5 4 3 2 1 0 MYA

MARY
LEAKEY'S
VIEW

AUSTRALOPITHECINES

HOMO LINE

LAETOLI FOSSILS

7 6 5 4 3 2 1 0 MYA

DONALD
JOHANSON'S
VIEW

AUSTRALOPITHECINES

HOMO LINE

HADAR FOSSILS

guing about names. They were really debating their different views of the Tree of Life. Did the genus *Homo* really stretch as far back as 3.5 million years in a single straight line? Or was Lucy a last common ancestor before the tree began to branch into many limbs, *Homo* and australopithecine?

Whether we call them *A. afarensis* or *Homo laetoli* or any

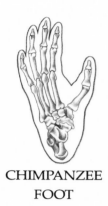

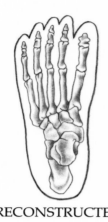

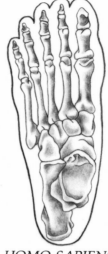

CHIMPANZEE
FOOT

RECONSTRUCTED
AUSTRALOPITHECUS
FOOT

HOMO SAPIENS
FOOT

one of the many names scientists might have used, it still does not tell us that much about how these creatures lived. From the examinations of the Laetoli and Afar fossil materials we know that the males were much larger than the females, up to one-third taller and more heavily built. Scientists wonder if this size difference might have affected how males and females interacted. Lucy stood about three and a half feet tall and weighed about sixty pounds. Her brow sloped back into a skull that held a brain about the size of an ape's.

Lucy's arms were longer than a modern human's and her legs were shorter. Her toes were long and curved, similar to chimps' toes, which are so good for grasping branches. She might have spent some time in the trees. These earliest hominids matured early. One way in which scientists can determine maturation is by examining the microstructure of the tooth enamel and determining the eruption age of teeth, or the time at which certain teeth break through the gums. In the fossil jaws of these early australopithecines adult teeth were often fully developed by the age of ten. A female could have her first child by the time she was eleven or twelve years old and death, if natural, occurred near forty. When Lucy died, she was about as mature as a twenty-year-old human today.

Mary Leakey wrote that often at dusk, after a long day in the field painstakingly excavating, or after long hours in the field lab studying the fossil evidence, she would walk out by herself and watch the sunset. The low slanting light would throw the footprints into sharp contrast with the ground—so sharp they almost seemed freshly made—and she could not help but wonder where these distant creatures were from and where they were going. She believed very deeply that they were human, on a uniquely human journey that eventually led directly to the emergence of modern man.

———

If we, too, were to walk out into the African dusk, we might imagine that this is a new grassland and that at its far edge is an ancient forest. Night passes. Dawn's milky shafts of light begin to penetrate the forest, revealing a group of apelike creatures foraging for figs in the dense ground vegetation of the forest. Many are crouching as they search for the sweet fruits, but occasionally they stand up to walk to another area nearby. As they stand up, the difference in size between the males and the females is noticeable.

A female who has found a patch thick with the fruits looks up warily as a male approaches. He notices how many she is finding. He takes several from her pile and begins eating them. She gathers up the remainder and scurries away toward the

very edge of the forest. There is a twisted tree. The lichen that used to grow on one side has been scoured off by wind and exposure, for although this tree used to be in the heart of the forest it is now at the edge facing the new and encroaching grassland. The young female puts her figs under some plants that grow at its base. Then, taking one fig in her mouth, she leaps toward a low branch. Wrapping her long fingers around the limb she swings her legs up easily. In a series of fluid, easy moves she ascends into the higher branches. She finds a comfortable spot where one branch joins with the trunk at an easy angle. She settles in, begins to eat. She looks to the grassland. She does not wonder. She does not dream. She likes the feel of the wind and the sun on her face.

She puts her hand on her belly. It feels different—round and hard—and something moves inside, but she does not know what it is, for she has never felt this before. She is eleven years old and this is her first time. The baby that will be born in a few months will never call her "mother," although it will know to look to her to be fed and touched and held. And she, the mother who will never be called mother, will know how to nurse the baby and care for it and love it wordlessly in a world that existed over three and a half million years ago.

A Manlike Ape or an Apelike Man?

The year is 1924, fifty years before Don Johanson's discovery of Lucy. It is a summer day, and within half an hour several guests are expected at the home of Dr. Raymond Dart, professor of anatomy at the University of Witwatersrand in Johannesburg, South Africa, for a wedding. He is to be the best man and has agreed to host the ceremony and reception at his home. As the guests arrive, Dart is in his bedroom half dressed, and instead of fixing his tie and pulling on his trousers he is rummaging through a box of rocks, chunks of limestone sent

to him from the Taung limeworks, a quarry where fossils have turned up. Although Dart's professional focus is the anatomy of modern human beings, his favorite hobby is collecting fossils. The wedding is actually the last thing on his mind even as the groom bangs on the door, telling him to hurry up. Dr. Dart has just found an incredibly shaped piece of limestone. To the untrained eye it is merely a roundish hunk, but to Dart it is immediately recognizable as an endocranial cast. Such a cast forms when a skull fills up with limestone, or some other sub-

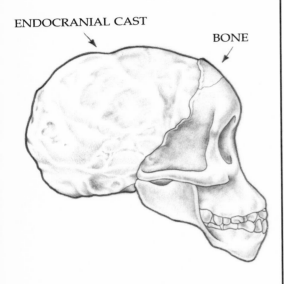

ENDOCRANIAL CAST   BONE

The Taung skull was found in two pieces embedded in a chunk of limestone. One piece contained facial bones and teeth. The other was a stone cast formed inside the missing fossil skull, which showed what the brain had looked like.

stance, which gradually solidifies and produces an exact replica of the brain that had vanished eons ago.

"I stood," Dart wrote in *Adventures with the Missing Link*, ". . . holding the brain as greedily as any miser hugs his gold. . . . Here, I was certain, was one of the most significant finds ever made in the history of anthropology."

As soon as the wedding guests had departed Dart was back examining the skull, turning it over in his hands. It was exceptionally small for a human skull. Could it be a baboon's? Dart didn't think so. The hole where the spinal cord entered the brain was at the bottom of the skull. This meant the creature walked upright. In animals that move on all fours the hole for the spinal column is toward the back of the skull. Dart stared at it, perplexed. The face and brain were so small, yet the canines were very humanlike. Was there such a thing as an erect walking ape? Or could this be the "missing link"—the creature that stood or perhaps stooped at the fork in the road between ape and man?

"A manlike ape?" asked one journalist.

"No, more an apelike man," Dart replied.

"Absolutely not! Never!" the scientific establishment cried. Its members had finally come around to Darwin's way of thinking, but most of them felt that if we had to share a common ancestor with the apes, it must have been a very special creature indeed—say, one with a nice, high-domed cranium, a fitting holder for that magnificent brain that would be human.

The problem with this creature of Dart's was that it resembled too nearly a chimpanzee. The top part of its skull sloped like a chimp's, and it had no chin. The brain capacity was scarcely one-third that of a person's today. And it was really small—the fossil of a child who had died very young.

66

YOUNG CHIMPANZEE

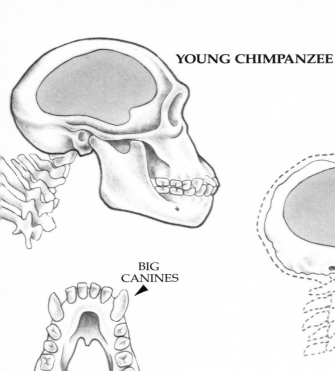

TAUNG CHILD

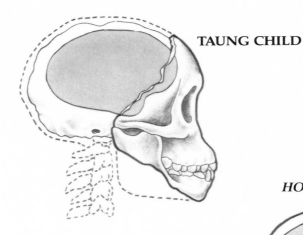

BIG
CANINES

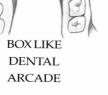

BOX LIKE
DENTAL
ARCADE

SMALL
CANINES

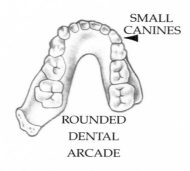

ROUNDED
DENTAL
ARCADE

HOMO SAPIENS **CHILD**

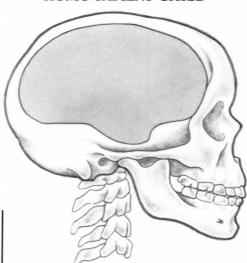

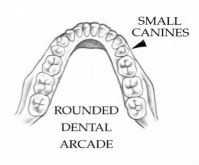

SMALL
CANINES

ROUNDED
DENTAL
ARCADE

Dart, in the tradition of all scientists who make exciting and important discoveries, gave the creature a long, fancy name—*Australopithecus africanus*, which roughly means ''southern ape from Africa.'' But the rest of the world laughed and called it simply the Taung baby.

People were outraged at the suggestion that our ancestor could have a monkey-size brain. One woman wrote a letter to Dart that expressed the feeling of the times:

''How can you, with such a wonderful gift of God-given genius—not the gift of a monkey, but a trust from the Almighty—become a traitor to your Creator by making yourself the active agent of Satan and his ready tool? . . . You with your splendid brain, God's gift to you, have become one of the Devil's best agents in sending seeking souls to grope in darkness.''

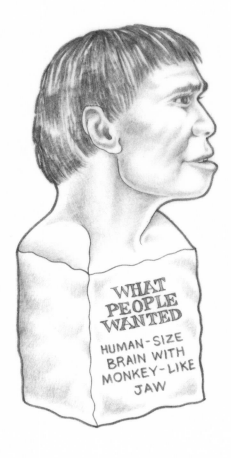

WHAT
PEOPLE
WANTED

HUMAN-SIZE
BRAIN WITH
MONKEY-LIKE
JAW

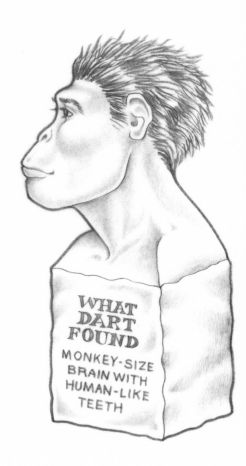

WHAT
DART
FOUND

MONKEY-SIZE
BRAIN WITH
HUMAN-LIKE
TEETH

Dart did not feel devilish at all. Nor did he feel he was groping in darkness. Dim regions of the past were becoming luminous as he worked meticulously for months, chipping away at the limestone consolidation of sand and rocks in which parts of the face and jaw were embedded. He was constantly comparing its features to those of apes as well as humans and guessed it to be about one million years old. "I grew prouder of my 'baby,' " he wrote. "Here was a creature which, in the exasperating fashion of children throughout the ages, was daring to vie with Man."

Other scientists were hoping that a more appropriate missing link might be found, preferably on European soil. As luck would have it, in 1912 such a creature had been discovered in a gravel pit near Piltdown, England. It became known as the "Piltdown Man." Its skull was shaped

Painting of Sir Arthur Keith and colleagues examining the Piltdown skull

like a human's and its jaw like an ape's. Nobody paid much attention to it at the time. But Sir Arthur Keith, a distinguished anatomist, was terribly exasperated that Dart's little monkey had dared claim human kinship. Indeed, he was downright snooty. "At most," he huffed, "it represents a genus in the chimpanzee or gorilla group. . . . The Taung child is much too late in the scale of time to have any place in man's ancestry."(While Dart called his find the Taung Baby, it became more commonly known as the Taung Child.) As far as Sir Arthur was concerned, the Taung child was just another ape. He seized upon Piltdown Man—such a sensible-looking fellow with such a respectably large brain! And he gave it a long fancy name after its discoverer, Charles Dawson—*Eoanthropus dawsoni*, or "Dawson's dawn man." It was

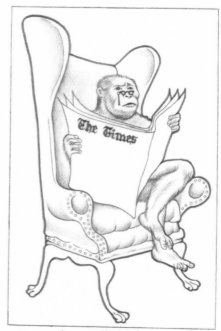

A very British ape-man

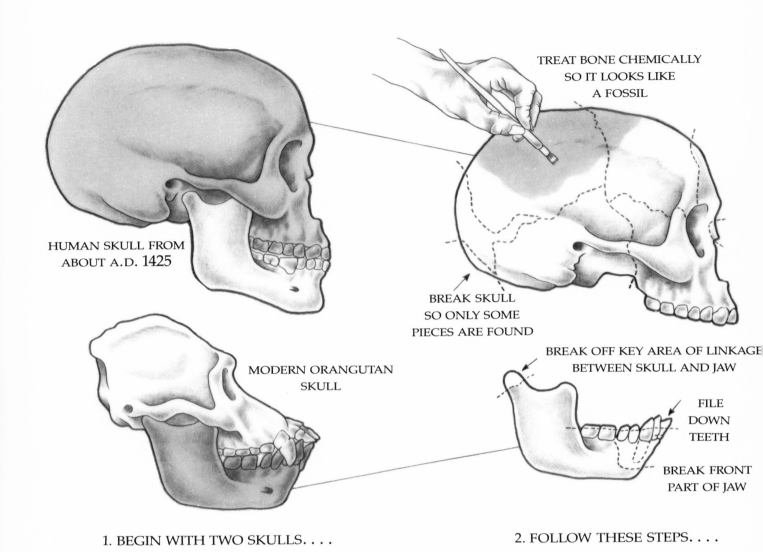

HUMAN SKULL FROM
ABOUT A.D. 1425

MODERN ORANGUTAN
SKULL

TREAT BONE CHEMICALLY
SO IT LOOKS LIKE
A FOSSIL

BREAK SKULL
SO ONLY SOME
PIECES ARE FOUND

BREAK OFF KEY AREA OF LINKAGE
BETWEEN SKULL AND JAW

FILE
DOWN
TEETH

BREAK FRONT
PART OF JAW

1. BEGIN WITH TWO SKULLS. . . .

2. FOLLOW THESE STEPS. . . .

easy for him and many others to pin their hopes on this elegant, intelligent, and very British ape-man.

The arguments over the Taung baby went on for twenty-five years, even after fossil remains from other australopithecines had been found. Finally scientists admitted what Dart had known all along, that australopithecines had more of a rounded dental arcade, like humans, and that their canines were blunt and small like those of hu-

PILTDOWN: HOW TO FAKE A FOSSIL SKULL

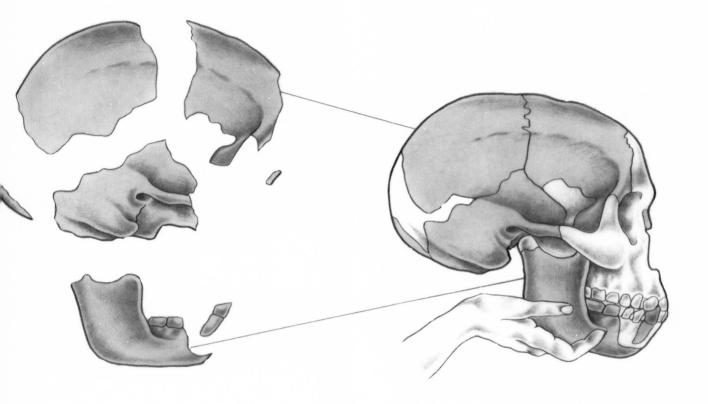

3. LEAVE PARTS TO BE DISCOVERED...

AND RECONSTRUCTED.

mans and not sharp and long like those of apes. The
molars, too, were worn to a flatter surface, more characteristic of human chewing patterns. At last, in 1950, Raymond Dart's Taung baby was declared a "potential"
human ancestor and admitted to the club—the hominid
club.

Shortly thereafter Piltdown Man was declared a fake.
By this time more accurate and complex tests were avail-

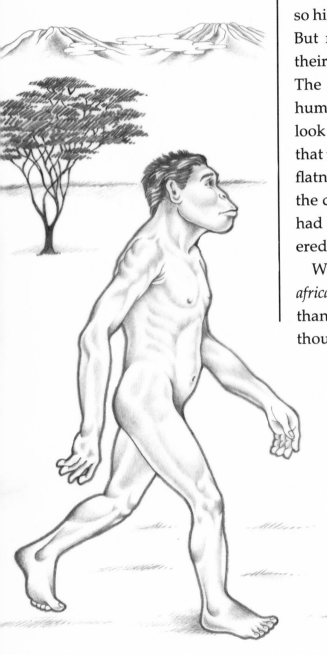

able for dating and evaluating fossils. It was discovered that Piltdown was a mere five hundred years old, which meant that he would have lived during the reign of Henry VI of England. In 1425 Henry VI was only four years old, so his uncle, the Duke of Gloucester, actually ran the show. But neither Henry, nor his uncle the Duke, nor any of their subjects looked a bit like Piltdown Man. No wonder. The "fossil" was an orangutan's jaw cemented on to a human's skull. The scientists who finally took a good hard look at Piltdown only needed a good microscope to see that the molars in the jaws had been filed down to a human flatness. The file marks were visible under the lens. And the dark color that gave the skull a nicely "antiqued" look had been painted on . . . by whom it was never discovered.

When the new dating techniques were applied to *A. africanus* it was found to be 2.5 million years old, more than a million years older than Dart himself had ever thought.

The Blossoming Tree of Life

It is difficult to imagine how beings who lived over two million years ago behaved. With so little evidence many myths have sprung up concerning early hominids.

A. africanus was called the "missing link." It is true he was "missing" for quite a while before Dart found him. However, "link" suggests a straight line reaching back through time, making it all too easy to imagine the missing link as something in between, less than a human but better than an ape—some creature that climbed down from the trees for a few hours each day and walked on two legs, but bent over slightly from the strain.

Back in the seventeenth century a famous English doctor, Edward Tyson, guessed that man had descended from apes. He imagined the perfect in-between creature—a pygmy chimpanzee. There are such animals as pygmy chimpanzees, but in a book on the subject the respected doctor showed the chimp walking with a cane!

Australopithecines are often pictured as slightly stooped, as if they were not used to walking fully erect or suffered from severe lower-back pain. There is absolutely no evidence to indicate that these hominids could not manage an upright walking posture. Perhaps we imagine them as slouched, knuckle-dragging ape-men because we believe them to be so inferior to ourselves. Most researchers still consider it possible that *A. africanus* (the Taung baby) was a link between *A. afarensis* (Lucy) and *Homo* (ourselves—from the Greek word that means "human" or "mankind"). Three other early hominids co-existed with *A. africanus* for different lengths of time. A little more than ten years after Dart found the Taung baby, his friend Robert Broom discovered a closely related but

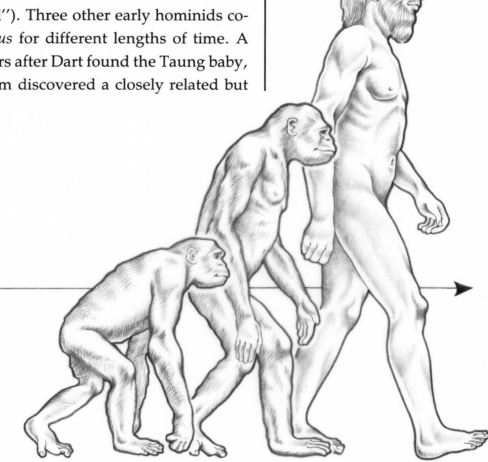

APE   A "MISSING LINK"?   *HOMO SAPIENS*

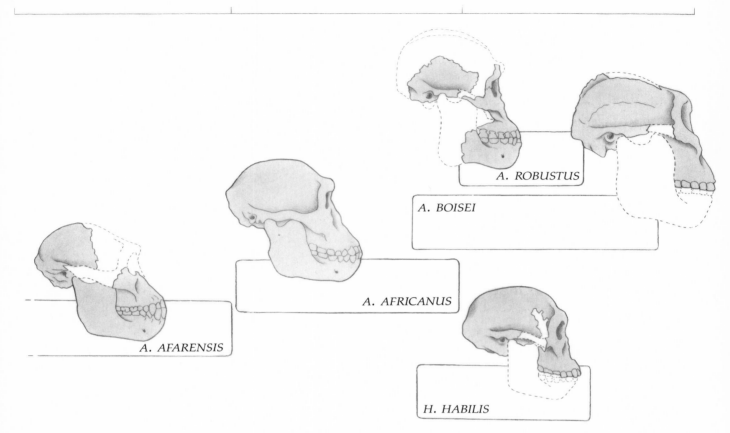

A. ROBUSTUS

A. BOISEI

A. AFRICANUS

A. AFARENSIS

H. HABILIS

much larger hominid which he named *Australopithecus robustus*. Then in 1959 Mary Leakey, who with her husband Louis had been working in East Africa for nearly thirty years, found a creature who was more massive still. Louis Leakey thought up a fancy name for this great find— *Zinjanthropus boisei* (*Zinj* means "East Africa," and *anthropus*, "man"). But they finally settled on *Australopithecus boisei* instead. *Boisei* was for Charles Boise, a man who had helped to finance many of the Leakeys' expeditions in Africa. The third early hominid was something new on the hominid scene: a larger-brained, tool-making creature who would be named *Homo habilis*, or "Handy Man." With all these variations of early hominids, the Tree of Life was blossoming into something more like a bush.

Early hominids were often misrepresented as bloodthirsty killers. Raymond Dart truly believed this. "They were murderers and flesh hunters," he wrote. " . . .their favorite tool was a bludgeon of bone." His evidence was a limestone cave in South Africa filled with smashed skulls and bones that looked as if they could have been used as clubs. Further examination suggested another possibility. Holes found in a fossilized skull matched perfectly the lower canines of a leopard's jaw found nearby. Leopards were known to drag their prey into trees to consume the flesh, dropping the bones and skull to the ground. Oftentimes there was a cave shaft beneath the very tree where the leopard had eaten its prey. The caves became catch basins for scraps from the leopard's meal. We now know that australopithecines were more likely to be the hunted than the hunter.

*Evidence against
Dart's theory*

A. boisei was also called Nutcracker Man, and with good reason: his huge molars—one inch in diameter—were terrific for chewing nuts, fibrous roots, and tubers. All of the australopithecines had large grinding teeth, which are just what is needed for a vegetarian diet. The cartoon image of a skulking, knuckle-dragging, club-toting thug does not match the reality that paleoanthropologists and archaeologists have been able to piece together. Australopithecines need to be appreciated not as steps to something better but as unique beings, specially suited for the time and the environment in which they lived—a time over two million years ago that made demands with which modern human beings might not have coped so well.

In Kenya there is a lake 155 miles long. On the map it looks like a jade-green whale swimming out of the Indian Ocean and slashing northward across Africa. Immense crocodiles swim in it. Herds of zebra and giraffe come to

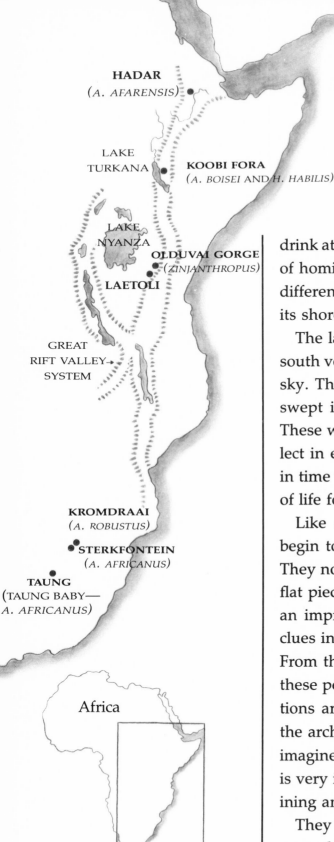

HADAR
(*A. AFARENSIS*)

LAKE
TURKANA

KOOBI FORA
(*A. BOISEI* AND *H. HABILIS*)

LAKE
NYANZA

OLDUVAI GORGE
(*ZINJANTHROPUS*)

LAETOLI

GREAT
RIFT VALLEY →
SYSTEM

KROMDRAAI
(*A. ROBUSTUS*)

STERKFONTEIN
(*A. AFRICANUS*)

TAUNG
(TAUNG BABY—
A. AFRICANUS)

Africa

Hominid fossil sites

drink at its shores, and its ancient sediments are a treasury of hominid fossils revealing that at one time at least two different kinds of hominids ranged and camped around its shores.

The lake is called Turkana. Beyond it to the north and south volcanoes once erupted, their plumes inscribing the sky. The ashes then cascaded down the steep cones and swept into the streams and rivers that ran to the lake. These waters carried ash and silt that would begin to collect in ever-deepening layers to form the sediments that in time would turn bone to stone and preserve the traces of life for the next two and a half million years.

Like detectives the scientists come to the lake—and begin to wonder. Was it the site of a prehistoric picnic? They note the pile of hippo bones, the stone flakes (small flat pieces chipped from a rock), several stone choppers, an impression of a fig leaf. The archaeologists look for clues in the trash and material remains from ancient life. From this they try to build a picture and figure out who these people were and how they lived. Often more questions are raised than are answered. That is often when the archaeologists and the paleoanthropologists begin to imagine. Imagining can help them to understand—but it is very important that scientists say when they are imagining and when they just plain know.

They know that *A. boisei* lived in the region of the jade-green lake. The fossil skulls of these australopithecines show flat and slightly concave faces with a bony ridge

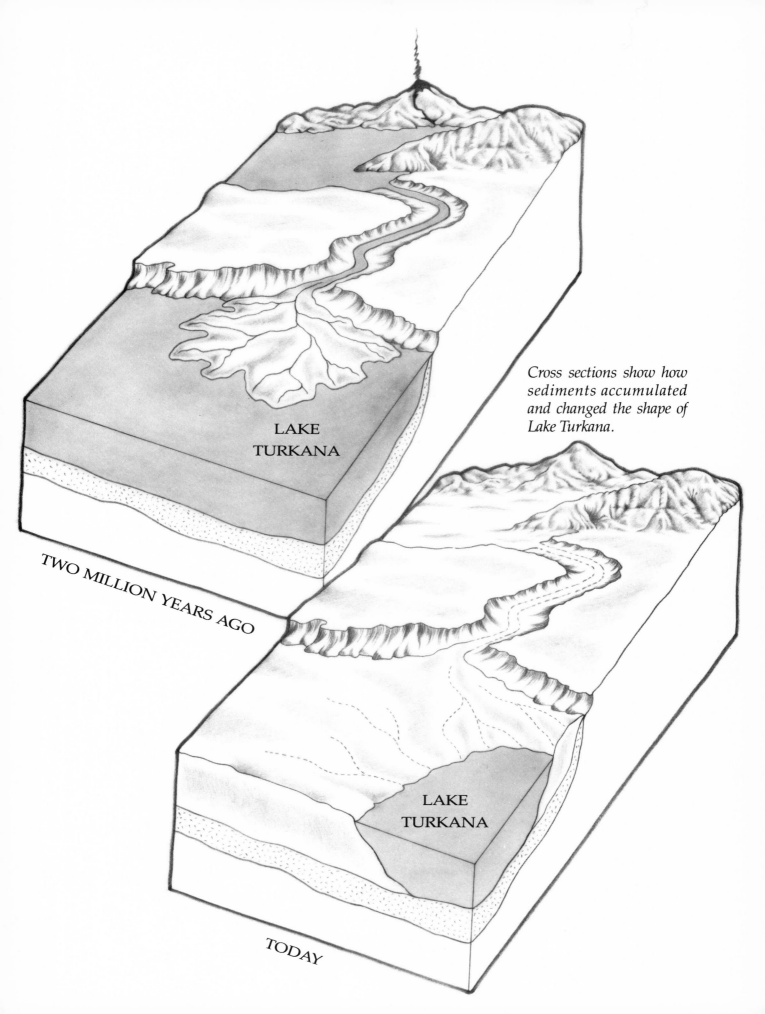

Cross sections show how
sediments accumulated
and changed the shape of
Lake Turkana.

LAKE
TURKANA

TWO MILLION YEARS AGO

LAKE
TURKANA

TODAY

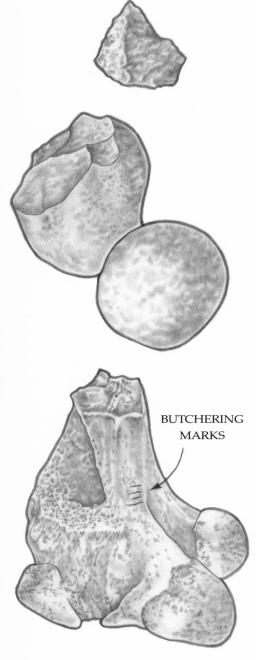

Flake, stone tools, and bone with butchering marks from Olduvai Gorge, associated with A. boisei

BUTCHERING
MARKS

running from front to back along the top of the skull. The ridge is called the *sagittal crest* and helped anchor their huge jaw muscles. There was a protruding ridge over the eye sockets and no real forehead. From studying the shape of the skull scientists can tell that the voice box, or larynx, in these hominids had not dropped down, as it has in modern human beings, and therefore was limited in the number of sounds it could produce. The voice box is still high in modern apes, and it is located high in human babies until they are three months old.

Scientists also know that *Homo habilis* lived in another region around Lake Turkana. Their bones were more delicate than those of australopithecines and their teeth were worn in a way that suggests they chewed meat as well as plant food. Their fossil remains have been found with the fossils of animals and a number of intriguing stone tools. Many of the animal remains have cut marks from having been butchered. Other bones are polished at the ends and are scratched on their surfaces. Perhaps they were used for digging roots and tubers, which were still a big part of the early hominid diet.

This is some of what scientists have discovered and know. Here is what they might imagine:

———————

It is a still, breathlessly hot day two million years ago. A small herd of gazelles dip into the water's edge for a drink, their delicate heads alert even as they drink. Their ears twitch, their eyes watch for the crocodiles that may be lurking in the shallows. Not far from the herd of gazelles a small band of creatures can be seen. They are short, the grown-ups not much bigger than sixth- or seventh-graders of today. The males are larger than

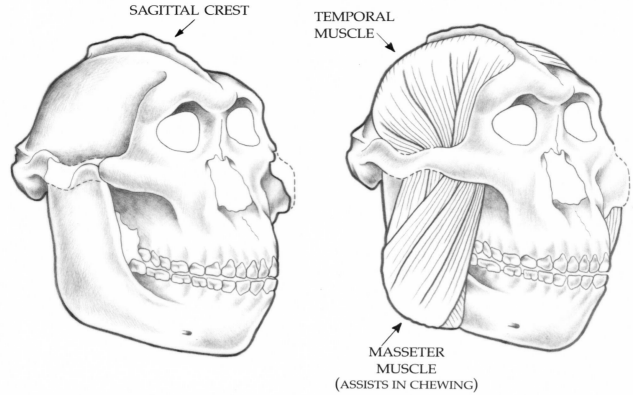

SAGITTAL CREST

TEMPORAL MUSCLE

MASSETER MUSCLE
(ASSISTS IN CHEWING)

ZINJANTHROPUS (A. BOISEI)

the females. Their heads appear small, their jaws huge. They seem to be moving away from the sandy shore into the deep fringe of grass and bush that is the savannah. A mother is crouched, digging with a stick for tubers. A baby sits on the ground near her, chewing on a thick tuber. Nearby a small girl of perhaps four or five dances around excitedly while her father wrestles with the prickly branch of a whistling thornbush for an ant gall that swells like a woody blister on the limb. The galls are edible. They eat these, along with insects and nuts and hard-shelled fruits and roots. They forage as they go. An older male hands something to a small child.

They take what they can find and occasionally crack a smooth pebble on another rock to make a

sharp edge. But it is not often that they think to make a tool, or plan to gather food in the morning for an evening meal. It is hard to save, to plan, to envision for a time that is not now. The group might sleep in the same place as the night before. Or they might not. They will not make a fire. They will not sing or whisper prayers. They communicate with sounds but not words. When these robust australopithecines go to sleep, if the lion prowls too near they will know what to do, and if the baby cries they will know how to give comfort. But they do not have weapons or lullabies in the night.

At a stream bed another group gathers. They are about the same size as the australopithecines, but their heads seem larger and their jaws smaller. There is no trace of the bony crest on their skulls. They are circling the carcass of a hippo, which collapsed and died in the stream very recently. The crocodiles have not come yet, nor have the lions or the hyenas. *Homo habilis* has arrived first. Some of them are looking for suitable stream cobbles or small rocks from which to make cutting tools. A boy and a girl remember a pile of lava cobbles upstream. They put down their leaf baskets, which contain some roots and tubers.

The members of this group will cut up the carcass with razor-sharp stones. They will eat some of the meat on the spot. The rest they will take back to a site where they have carried stone material useful for making tools. Here the animal parts can be more thoroughly butchered.

At night they will eat more of the meat, cutting

it with sharp stones. With rough round stones they may pulverize some hard nuts to a paste and—who knows?—stick on a passing beetle or top it with a grub or a berry. It is, after all, a feast— a celebration. But there is no music or dancing, no speeches, no toasts. When they sleep, there's a chance that they dream. Their dreams will remain a mystery to us, for unlike stones and bones they will leave no trace. And if these creatures really do dream, will their dreams thrill them, astound them, and frighten them as our dreams sometimes do?

————————

These two kinds of hominids lived separately yet at the same time near Lake Turkana. For some reason the robust australopithecines "dead-ended" in terms of evolution. Their lineage stopped and could not be traced after 1.5 million years ago. *Homo habilis*, the hominid at the stream bed, handy with his stone-cutting tools as he stripped meat from the hippo bones, was destined to become the cause of another big argument among scientists.

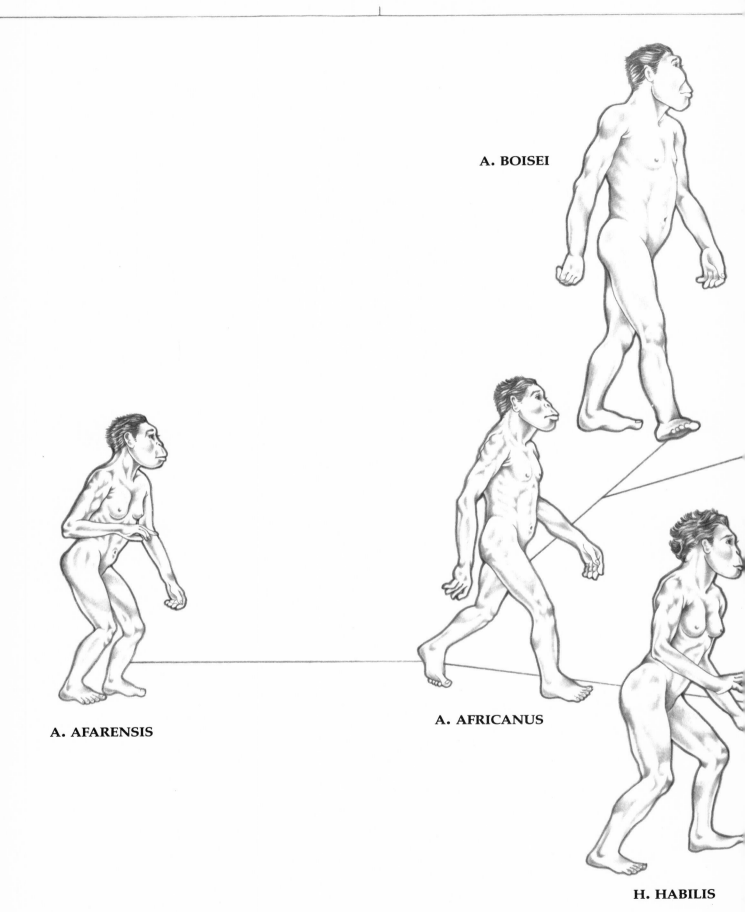

A. BOISEI

A. AFARENSIS

A. AFRICANUS

H. HABILIS

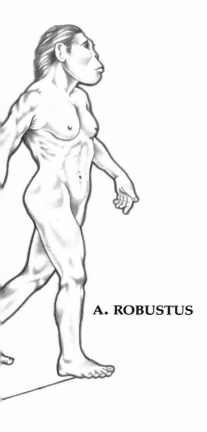

A. ROBUSTUS

?

THE EVOLUTIONARY PATH

How the different hominid species related to each other and when each first appeared in time.

The Remarkable Leakeys

The child of English missionaries, Louis Leakey was born in 1903, in a grass hut in the small hamlet of Kabete. The Kikuyu warriors of East Africa had awaited his birth eagerly outside the hut, for they had never before seen a white baby. It was said that when the tribal elder came into the hut to greet the newborn infant, he imagined a black baby with a white face.

Louis Leakey would always feel more African than English, and he would devote his life to searching for hominids in the Great Rift Valley of East Africa. He was a

Louis and Mary Leakey, with a skull 600,000 years old.

paleoanthropologist, a scholar, a showman, and a free spirit. With his wife, Mary, he made international news. He inspired governments and institutions such as the National Geographic Society to pour money into research on the origins of our human family.

Although the Leakeys often traveled all over the world, they lived and raised their children in Africa. Jonathan, Richard, and Philip Leakey often accompanied their parents on archaeological expeditions. A favorite trip was from their home in Nairobi to the islands in the middle of Lake Victoria. Victoria is an enormous lake that spills over the borders into three countries—Kenya, Tanzania, and Uganda. The Leakeys would drive all through the day

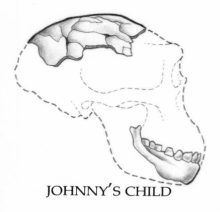

JOHNNY'S CHILD

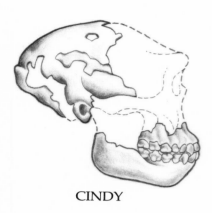

CINDY

TWIGGY

and deep into the night. There were no fast food restaurants. There were no public rest rooms or gas stations at regular intervals. There was just Africa.

Close to midnight they would arrive at the eastern shore of the lake. Sleepy children and provisions would be packed onto a boat called the *Miocene Lady*. They would then set off toward the islands. Richard Leakey remembers that the highlight of their arrival would be the first swim in the lake. "We were taken ashore in a small dinghy and my father would carefully scan the bay with his binoculars before blasting off with both barrels of his shotgun into the water where we were to bathe. As soon as the echoes of the blast died away, we were allowed to rush into the water and have our swim while father stood guard. The noise was to scare the many crocodiles." Had any of the Leakeys been eaten by crocodiles the collected fossil record would be poorer, for this remarkable family has been in search of early humans for over fifty years.

When he was a teenager in Tanzania, Jonathan Leakey found a jaw belonging to a young child. It became known as "Johnny's Child." His father helped him excavate some hand bones and skull fragments that belonged to the same creature.

Louis Leakey observed from these few fragments that Johnny's Child had some ability to manipulate small objects. After Johnny's Child had been found, fragments belonging to another hominid turned up. There was not much: a patch of skull, parts of an upper jaw, some teeth, and a lower jaw. The evidence was so fragmentary it was hard to tell whether the pieces belonged to a female or male. But the Leakeys named it Cinderella, perhaps in honor of the smashed glass slipper, and called it "Cindy" for short.

Then came George. "Poor George," Mary Leakey called him. He really was smashed. He was found late one afternoon when it was becoming too dark to begin the delicate task of chipping the skull out of the rock chunk in which it was embedded. By the next morning a herd of cattle had trampled George to smithereens. All that was left were some skull pieces and teeth.

"Twiggy," although not crushed by cattle, had been squashed flat by the immense pressure of the rocks above it and thus was named for a very skinny English fashion model.

These four fossils were old, almost two million years old according to the potassium-argon dating, and they were human, or at least directly in the line that led to humans. Of this the Leakeys were convinced. Therefore the fossils were assigned to the genus *Homo*. Louis Leakey, along with two other scientists, Philip Tobias and John Napier, gave them the name *Homo habilis*, remembering the special hand of Johnny's Child that could grasp small objects.

Louis Leakey believed they were human for several reasons: their brain capacity was larger than that of the australopithecines, their jaws and teeth were more like those of modern humans, and their skulls had a different, more human shape. And they seemed to have the ability to make tools. He declared *H. habilis* "the father of modern man."

But there were people who disagreed. Many thought that the skimpy crushed fossil fragments did not provide enough evidence to say that *H. habilis* was a truly different genus. The critics believed that when all the parts of the jigsaw puzzle came together, George, Cindy, Twiggy, and Johnny's Child would look an awful lot like australopithecines.

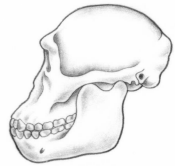

A. AFRICANUS

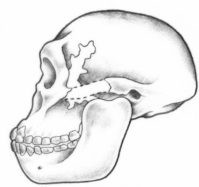

H. HABILIS

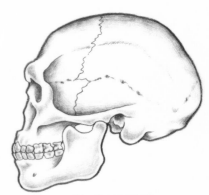

H. SAPIENS

Compare the shapes of the teeth, jaws, and skulls of H. habilis *and* A. africanus *and notice how different they are.*

"*Homo habilis* should be sunk," one critic said. He did not mean that the fossils should be destroyed—just the special category with its elaborate name. But Louis Leakey hadn't thought up the name to amuse himself. Naming is part of the process of describing and measuring and evaluating a fossil, which is why Don Johanson and Mary Leakey argued so passionately about the identity of Lucy and the makers of the Laetoli footprints. They also understood that to name something helps people to understand its meaning better. The trouble was most scientists seemed to disagree with Leakey's meaning.

One of Louis Leakey's many interests, perhaps his most ardent, was the near side of the fork, the side on which could be found the most humanlike of our ancestors and the line of hominids that had produced us—modern *Homo sapiens*. Leakey felt that the *Homo* line could be pushed back, further back than anyone had previously dared or dreamed—perhaps even to four million years ago. Scientists continued to insist that the evidence was too patchy, so Johnny's Child, Twiggy, George, and Cindy existed in a shadowy back alley for homeless hominids until 1972, when one of the most important hominid fossils ever was found. It was as perfect a specimen as one could hope for and it was called by its catalog number, 1470—a stubby little four-digit number for such a brilliant discovery!

Richard Leakey was in his twenties when a member of his team named Bernard Ngeneo found the shattered skull in a steep wild gully in East Turkana. It took days to excavate the fragments, and Richard's wife, zoologist Meave Leakey, spent six weeks reconstructing the skull. Only the lower jaw was missing. Richard Leakey placed it firmly in the genus *Homo*.

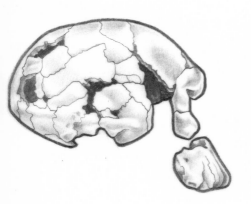 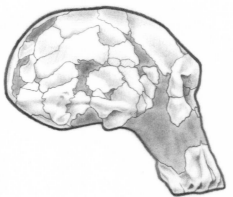 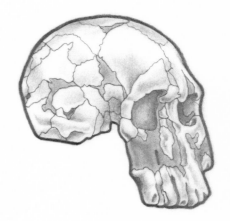

At first 1470 was dated close to 2.6 million years old. The date was later adjusted to 1.9 million years. According to most scientists, it was definitely *Homo*. It had a high-domed skull more delicate than the australopithecines' and with a decidedly larger brain capacity. With the discovery of such a complete specimen as 1470, the case for *H. habilis* was made and Twiggy, George, Cindy, and Johnny's Child stepped out of the shadows and were accepted as valid examples of the species. Louis Leakey died shortly after his son's brilliant discovery.

Mirror, mirror, on the wall, who is the most human of them all? Do measurements alone make one creature *Homo* and another australopithecine? An average modern human brain has a cranial capacity of about 1,400 cubic centimeters—1470's was just over half that, and *A. africanus*'s brain capacity was far less. Hominids have evolved toward larger brains, but we know that brain size is not the only measure of intelligence. Interior organization, the "wiring" or circuitry, is equally important in controlling the brain function, and so the person with the bigger head is not necessarily the brighter person.

Hominids in the genus *Homo* have a brain capacity of at least 600 centimeters and the ability to make tools. But

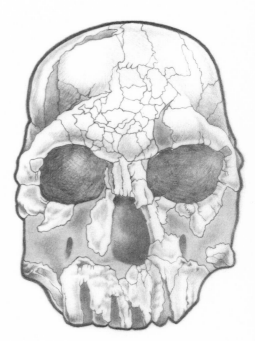

RECONSTRUCTION OF SKULL 1470

scientists have never pinpointed precisely what a human *is*. Perhaps it is not an issue scientists alone can settle. Nonetheless, at some arbitrary point certain hominids are deemed to be in the *Homo* line. It is almost as if there is some imaginary hallway through which they can pass into humanness.

Dr. Dubois's "Missing Link"

One hundred years ago scientists were still struggling with the revolutionary ideas put forth by Darwin. Hominid fossils had been found in France and Germany. But these were fossils of people who had lived tens of thousands of years before. To imagine that the human race might be hundreds of thousands of years old was almost impossible. Nobody had tracked that deeply into time. But in the late nineteenth century scientists were forced to consider the lower end of the chain and the so-called missing links that might lead to those extinct apes so "closely allied to gorillas and chimpanzees" that Darwin had written about.

One of these persons was a Dutch doctor named Eugene Dubois. In the 1880s he stopped doctoring to begin his search for the missing link. Dubois was a true "chain" thinker. He, like so many others, had misinterpreted Darwin to mean that apes and man existed in a direct relationship to one another as grandparent to grandchild, whereas Darwin had meant that apes and man shared a common ancestor and thus were related more like cousins. Dubois surmised, erroneously, that the link would be a creature half ape and half man. So he felt the logical place to go was Sumatra, where it was known that orangutans lived. (*Orangutan* comes from the Malaysian words for "man of the forest.") With any luck he was convinced he could find a very old fossil—the missing link.

Luck did not come exactly as Dubois had anticipated. He excavated for two years in Sumatra with little success and then contracted malaria and went to Java to recover. In Java he began working on a bend in the Solo River. He was finding many fossils—not precisely the kind he was looking for, but they were promising. The government provided him with convict labor, and soon after Dubois was shocked to discover that the convicts were stealing the fossils as fast as they found them to sell to Chinese traders, who ground the "dragon bones" into powder for medicines. Although there is no record of what Dubois said when he found out about this sideline activity, we can imagine his horror.

Eugene Dubois

———

"Dragon bones!" The Dutch doctor's face flushed a deep crimson. He blinked at his foreman in disbelief. "They think *these* are dragon bones!" He

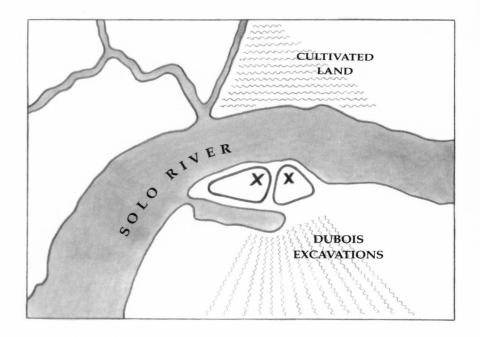

was nearly screaming as he held up a thighbone in his right hand.

"No! No!" the foreman said patiently, as if trying to explain to a child. "The prisoners don't think they are really dragon bones. They know what they are. They know, but they don't care."

Dr. Dubois decided to try another approach.

"Then who could possibly want to buy such ancient bones?"

"Chinese traders. They grind them up into powder."

"Into powder?" Dubois said weakly and mopped his brow.

"Yes, into powder to sell to Chinese people."

"For whatever purpose?"

"To eat."

"To eat!" Now the doctor looked positively ill.

"Yes. Powerful medicine. Cures many things. Good love potion, too."

Dubois, still weak from his illness, might have felt a malarial sweat begin to creep over his body. Next it would be the chills and who knew—maybe these thugs would try to sell him dragon powder to cure his fever!

We do not know if the beleaguered doctor really said any of these things, but we do know that he felt he had to stop the stealing of these fossil bones for "medicines" and "love potions." He managed to do this with the help of the local government, and finally, in 1892 and 1893, he began to uncover the most promising fossils of all: first a tooth, next a primate skull, and then a thighbone. After a careful examination of the thighbone, Dubois concluded that this creature was an upright walking ape who very much resembled a man. He called it *Pithecanthropus erectus*, which means "upright ape-man."

Dubois expected to return in glory, but instead many critics belittled his "missing link." They said the leg bone was "too modern" and many thought he had accidentally put it together with an ordinary ape's skull. However, Sir Arthur Keith, the fearsome head of the anthropological establishment in England who was later to give Raymond Dart so much trouble, felt that Dubois had misread these fossils from Java and that this creature was indeed human, not a manlike ape or a missing link, either. Dubois became so embittered by the controversy that he "re-buried" his fossils under the floorboards of his dining room and would not let anyone else see them!

The identity of *P. erectus* was debated for many years, for the story of humankind is one that must be told slowly and painstakingly. The earth does not yield more than a few sentences at one time, and it took almost fifty years

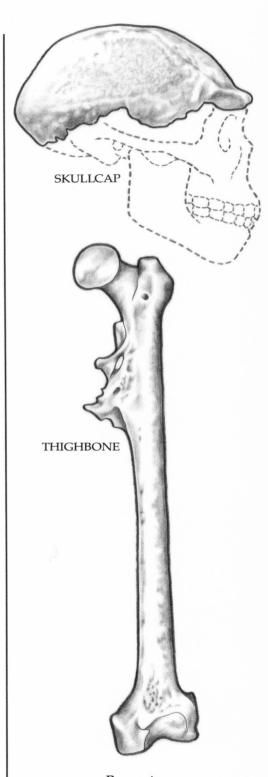

SKULLCAP

THIGHBONE

P. erectus

99

for the chapter on *Homo erectus* to be read and understood. Sir Arthur Keith was proven to be right. Java Man, as *P. erectus* was sometimes called, was human. And with legs that were identical to a modern human's, near-human teeth, and a skull that was like a human's except for its thick, dense bone, what an interesting member of the human family he was!

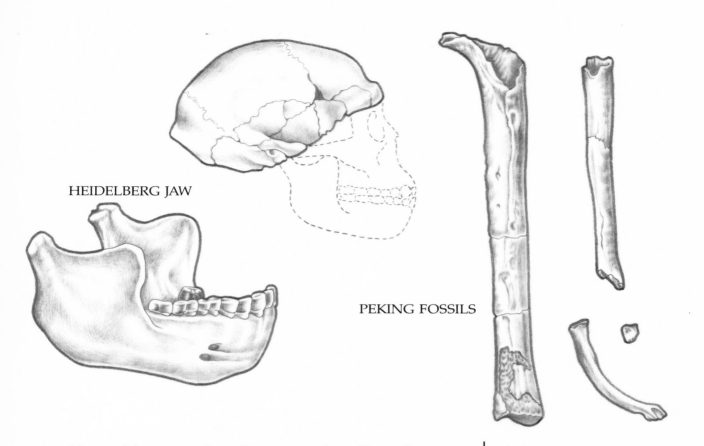

HEIDELBERG JAW

PEKING FOSSILS

Skullcap and its reconstruction, thighbone, upper armbone, collarbone, and wristbone of H. erectus

New evidence continued to accumulate. From Germany came Heidelberg Man, later followed by Peking Man, which was discovered in a cave in northern China. Each one was slightly different, but each was recognized as belonging to the genus *Homo*. It was finally decided that in spite of their variations, they were of the same species. So Java Man and Peking Man and finally Heidelberg Man were all given the same name—*Homo erectus*, or "upright man." They might have been nicknamed "Traveling Man" or "Traveling Woman," for *H. erectus* was the first hominid to migrate from Africa into Europe and Asia.

The oldest *H. erectus* fossil was found in East Africa. It was dated as 1.6 million years old. *H. erectus* lived alongside *A. robustus* and *A. boisei* for many thousands of years. Then some of them left the warmth and abundance of Africa and migrated north, where they had to learn to adapt to much harsher climates in order to survive. This

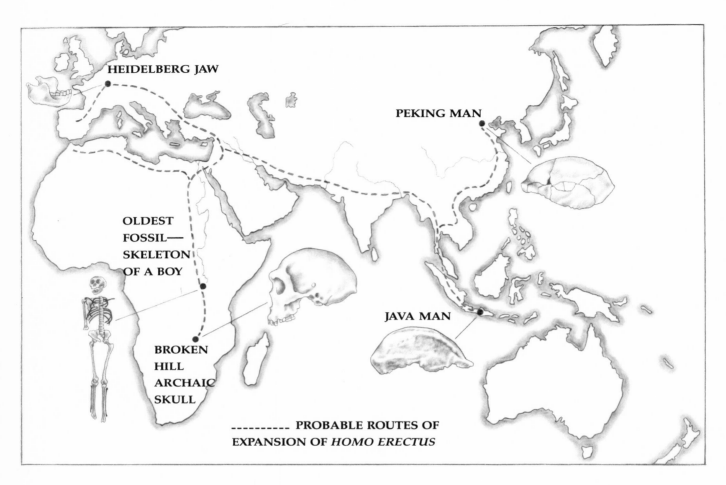

HEIDELBERG JAW

PEKING MAN

OLDEST
FOSSIL—
SKELETON
OF A BOY

JAVA MAN

BROKEN
HILL
ARCHAIC
SKULL

---------- PROBABLE ROUTES OF
EXPANSION OF *HOMO ERECTUS*

they did admirably well.

Until *H. erectus* most of what archaeologists dug up and examined were bones—hominid and animal. Now the first objects made by early people were entering the archaeological record. Stone tools had appeared before, as long ago as two million years, but never in such number and as consistently. Often they were discovered at campsites or in caves that had been occupied for a long time. Scientists were uncovering a variety of stone tools at every campsite—choppers, scrapers, blades, and, most interestingly, hand axes, pear-shaped tools with two sharp edges. These tools could work wood, scrape hides, butcher meat, and cut plants. And for warmth and perhaps cooking *H. erectus* had the use of fire—charcoal fragments and burned bones have also been found throughout Europe and Asia where this hominid lived.

H. erectus did not, however, as some have suggested, migrate to Asia and Europe to "get educated." One man who calls himself a scientist made the racist comparison of Africa to a kindergarten and Europe to a more advanced school. This is simply untrue. *H. erectus* did not leave Africa to get smart. Many did not leave at all. Whether they settled in Europe or Asia, they are all considered to be the same species. The wide geographic spread of *H. erectus*'s presence shows how resourceful and imaginative these early people could be.

H. erectus were taller than *Homo habilis*. They averaged five-and-a-half feet tall or a bit more. Their brains were larger—about two-thirds the size of ours. They were not as heavily built as *A. robustus*. Their faces were less jutting than those of *H. habilis* or any of the australopithecines. Their cheek teeth, those teeth that grow along the insides of the cheeks, were smaller, like those of modern humans, but their chins still seemed to pull back so that they were almost chinless. These hominids had one very distinctive feature—a long, low, heavy brow ridge that almost seemed to cast their eyes in shadow.

From the evidence of their living sites and their stone-tool technology, which were more advanced than either those of the australopithecines or *H. habilis*, it can be guessed that these people were more capable than any before them of keeping images in mind, so that tools could be made to a remembered pattern. They lived together in groups and possibly hunted large animals, which would require a high level of communication. One important hunting tool is missing from their tool kit (a *tool kit* is the

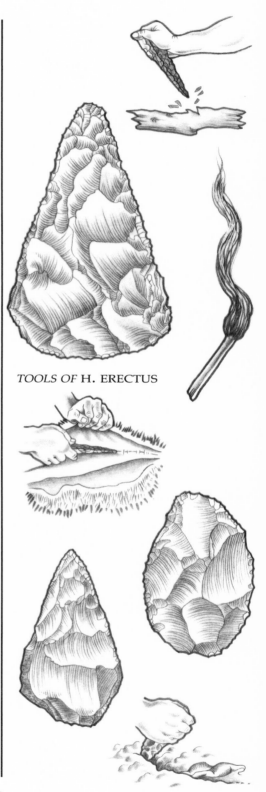

TOOLS OF H. ERECTUS

103

number of tools that were made)—hafted blades, or blades that are mounted onto a piece of wood like a spear. Perhaps hand axes were thrown like a discus, or perhaps *H. erectus* mostly butchered animals already dead or dying. However, we can imagine with a fair amount of certainty that 600,000 years ago elephants on occasion did get stuck in the mud and possibly, the meat having been stripped away and brought back to the campsite, there might be a reenactment of this exciting event, which in the telling is a kind of art.

———————

Imagine a large overhanging rock cliff that forms a natural roof. The low-angled slants of dawn light pierce the shadowy void beneath the roof, revealing the first human stirrings of a new day. The embers of the previous night's fire are poked into renewed life. Several people emerge from the shelter. Some sit near the fire. One draws a hot cobble from the embers with a stick and then, using a fragment of hide as a mitt, places it into a very large bowl made from the skull of a mammoth. The mammoth bowl has just been filled with liquid from a bag made out of the waterproof stomach of a bison.

As dawn melts into morning the people divide into smaller groups. Two children of nine or ten, a boy and a girl, follow a woman to a grove of trees where the tools are made. The ground is littered with stone fragments and flakes of rocks. The stone tools have been worked differently from those of earlier hominids. No longer are there the simple chunky rock cores and crudely shaped choppers for banging downward or ham-

mering or pulverizing. Only a few flakes had been removed from those older choppers to fashion them. The tools made by this group of *Homo erectus* have been worked on both sides, or bifacially.

The girl picks up a teardrop-shaped rock that she started to work on the day before. She is ready to finish it off now. Yesterday she used a chunky hammer stone to shape it roughly into the teardrop—a popular shape for hand axes. Now she picks up another tool, a baton of hard wood that has been specially made to use for this finishing work. She begins to strike off thin chips from the edge of her stone teardrop. In another few minutes she will have a sharp, straight-edged cutting tool.

The boy picks a rock from a nearby pile. The rock has an angled edge called a *platform*. In his left hand he holds a hammer stone that has already been split and shows a cutting edge. He brings the hammer stone down sharply against the platform of the rock. Nothing happens. The woman makes a low sound. The boy looks up. She hands him a sharp pointed bone and makes a gesture. The boy looks longingly at the woman's hammer stone. The woman makes another more abrupt sound and gestures toward the bone. "Use it," she seems to say with sound and gesture. The boy does. In a series of small pressure strokes he chips away at the platform. He strikes off two flakes from one side, then turns the rock over and repeats the process. While striking on one side he keeps a picture in his mind's eye of the other side.

If he can keep his mind's eye and his real eye on his working hands, in a few minutes he will have turned the rock into a sharp tool with a sharp, ragged edge.

At the rock shelter four or five children all under the age of four watch as their mothers walk down a well-worn path with baskets. Another group, mostly men and young boys, heads off in another direction. They carry with them close-range killing tools—blades, a bag of throwing rocks, some pointed sticks, but no spears or javelins with mounted stone points. If they are lucky they may find an elephant caught in the mud, or a dead deer. But they will keep a sharp eye out for small game they can kill by hand or with the quick, accurate throw of a rock.

That evening the band gathers once more around the fire. The sounds are lively and hands gesture rapidly. A young boy crouches on all fours and wiggles his nose just like the rabbit that he and his older brother almost caught that morning. The older brother steps out. He begins to reenact the morning scene. Down on his belly he scrambles toward the make-believe rabbit. The small boy turns abruptly and leaps in a smooth curve over his brother's head. The band roars with laughter.

When the laughter subsides they break up to head for their sleeping places in the shelter. The girl who was making stone tools that morning lingers by the fire. It is a clear starry night—the first in several days. She can see the great fixed star of the north. The girl feels her breath become

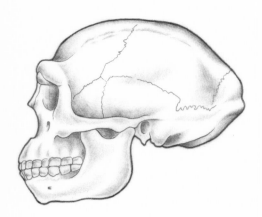

H. ERECTUS SKULL

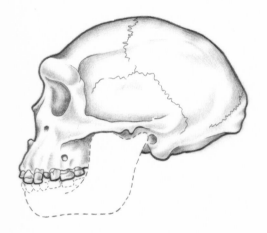

ARCHAIC SKULL FROM
BROKEN HILL, AFRICA

quiet and lock in her throat as a sense of mystery and awe fills her. She might have a religion, but its name and signs have not yet been carved or painted or made visible in stone. Perhaps these symbols are still buried deep in the minds of the band. As she turns from the star-channeled sky, she stares briefly into the fire. In the flames she sees a shape. It reminds her of a new shape she wants to try tomorrow at the grove of the tool-maker—a new kind of cleaver that will fit her hand better. She will go to sleep with the shape of the flame in her mind's eye, and tomorrow, a new day, she will try to turn the flame into stone—a new stone tool.

———————

Homo erectus first appeared in the fossil record about 1.6 million years ago and persisted until at least 300,000 years ago—a long run on the evolutionary calendar. Those who followed *H. erectus* had larger skulls and thinner bones, yet the tools they used remained pretty much the same. They have been called "transitional" and "archaic" human beings. They were probably ancestral to modern humans, but no one is quite sure how they related to the hominids who were coming next: *Homo sapiens*.

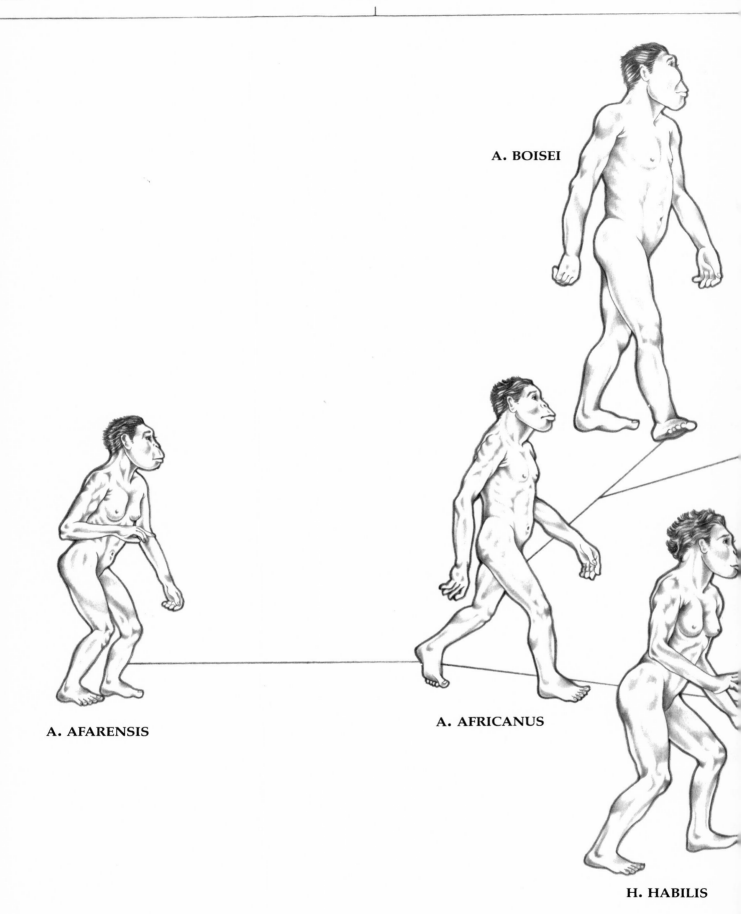

A. BOISEI

A. AFRICANUS

A. AFARENSIS

H. HABILIS

THE EVOLUTIONARY PATH

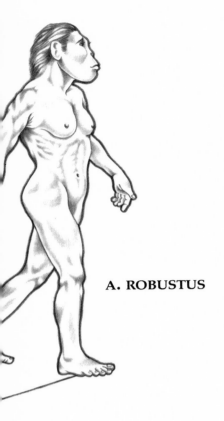

A. ROBUSTUS

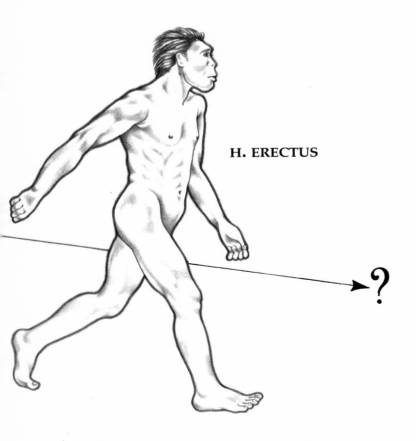

H. ERECTUS

?

The Riddle of the Neanderthals

Death often tells a story. At the time he died, the old man had been suffering from severe hip arthritis. The vertebrae in his spine had deteriorated. His gums were diseased and he had lost most of his teeth. He was, in short, a wreck. Most likely he walked with great difficulty. He could not hunt or chew food. And yet he lived to be an old man of forty-one or forty-two. Clearly his fellows must have cared for him. He is called by archaeologists the Old Man of La Chapelle aux Saints, the village in France where his fossil remains were found buried in a grave.

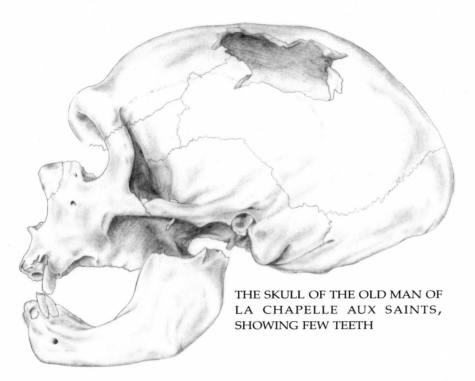

THE SKULL OF THE OLD MAN OF
LA CHAPELLE AUX SAINTS,
SHOWING FEW TEETH

At another site in France, the fossilized bones of an eighteen-year-old boy were discovered. He had been carefully placed on his side, his head resting on a pile of flaked flints, his arm beneath his head as if he were sleeping.

Site after site has revealed the first evidence of burial within the family of humankind. In 1950 a burial site was discovered in the Zagros mountains of northern Iraq in a cave called Shanidar. Pollen grains were found under the remains of an early man. It seemed to scientists that they were in some kind of pattern, as if flowers had been carefully arranged under the man's body. This was a wonderfully exciting notion, but further research revealed that the pollen grains could have been brought in by the bees that live in caves around Shanidar, or by other means. It was probable that the scientists saw in the pollen a significance that wasn't there. But that didn't detract from the importance of finding evidence of a purposeful burial 60,000 years before.

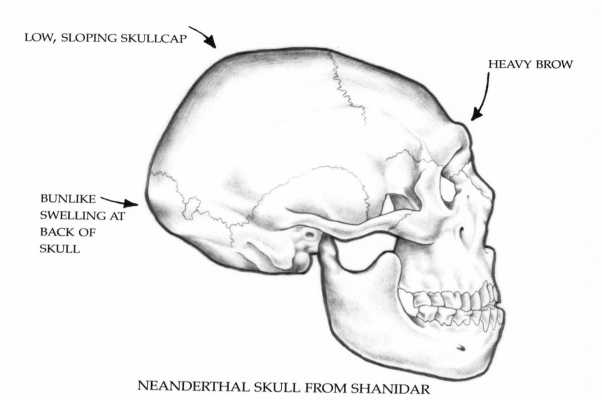

LOW, SLOPING SKULLCAP

HEAVY BROW

BUNLIKE SWELLING AT BACK OF SKULL

NEANDERTHAL SKULL FROM SHANIDAR

These fossils of Shanidar and La Chapelle aux Saints, as well as those of the teenage boy, all belong to a group of primitive human beings called *Homo sapiens neanderthalensis* ("wise man from the Neander Valley"). When the first Neanderthal fossils were found in the Neander Valley in Germany in 1856, they were greeted with dismay and ridicule. Could this creature have cared for its elderly and practiced some form of ritual burial? Its heavy brow and low, sloping skullcap, the bunlike swelling on the back of its skull, and its thick and curved limb bones were thought to belong to some apelike creature who could hardly be an ancestor of ours. If this creature was human, then it was a misfit, a freak of some sort. Here is a short list of some of the names this creature was called by several scientists and newspapers of that time:

"A poor idiotic hermit."

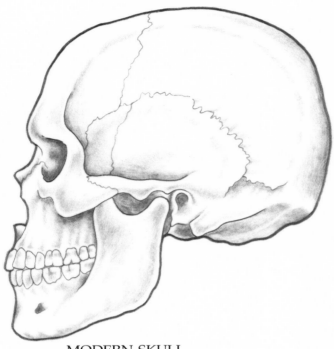

MODERN SKULL

An outdated reconstruction of a Neanderthal

"A pathological idiot."

"A member of a 'savage race.' "

"A dim-witted brute."

On the slightly more complimentary side, it was proposed by a Dr. Mayer of Bonn that the creature was a Mongolian cossack who had deserted the army, or perhaps a refugee from Noah's flood. Of course, it was none of these. Through archaeological evidence, we see in the Neanderthals the first signs of symbolic thought and a spiritual life.

The Neanderthals lived during one of several ice ages that have punctuated the past million years. The periods between these ice ages are called *interglacials*. We are living in one now. The Neanderthals of western Europe were separated from others of their species by the ice age that lasted from 70,000 to 35,000 years ago. Although Europe

115

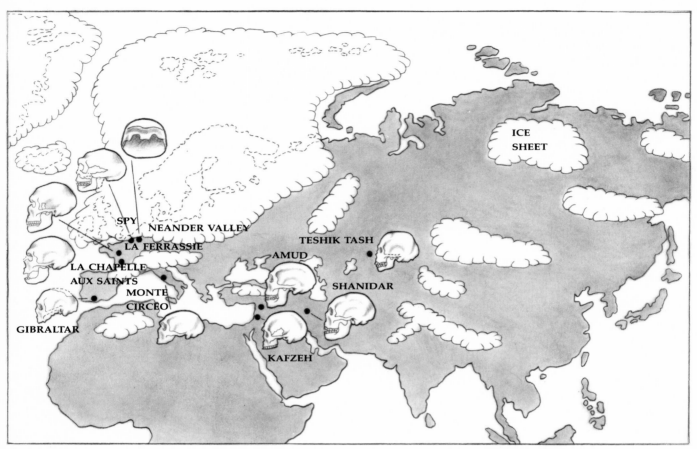

The spread of H. sapiens neanderthalensis

wasn't totally covered with ice, it had a very cold and harsh climate. The Neanderthals moved in bands, returning to camps each season where the gathering or game was good. Sometimes they built crude structures of branches or skin. Most often they lived in caves for protection from the cold.

They were brave hunters, but they probably relied more on gathering and scavenging for food. They were also clever toolmakers. Their tool kit included sixty different tools with many smaller, more refined implements for such specialized work as carpentry, sewing, and prepar-

116

ing hides. Excavations from various sites have turned up scrapers, blades, and points for hafting onto spears as well as "denticulated," or saw-toothed, implements.

Early hominids often relied on luck and opportunism for survival. Scientists imagine that early fire users like *Homo erectus* took advantage of fire when they found it during forest fires or when trees were hit by lightning. The coals would be gathered, protected, and nurtured into new flame.

The Neanderthals were different. They could make and control fire, organize hunts, store food for the coldest months, on occasion build crude living shelters, and envision and make new implements. The "tool" that probably helped them the most in doing all these things was language. It is one thing to imagine the shape of a tool. It is still another to describe its shape and how it will work and give it a name. To name is not simply to know but to communicate and to invite others to share and learn— whether a strategy of the hunt or how to keep fire alive or where to find a remembered living site. Language is invisible, but from the fossil record it is clear that the mind that created this world of complex physical tools and communal action was surely capable of some kind of speech.

In a cave called Drachenloch, which means "dragon's lair," archaeologists discovered an odd arrangement of bones. As the excavations proceeded, a rock "chest" was found buried in the floor. It contained seven bear skulls and stacks of leg bones. Each bear skull faced the mouth of the cave. It seemed possible that the numerous arrangements of bones were intentional and symbolic and most likely connected with some ritual. The exact ritual might remain unknown, but it could be imagined. And

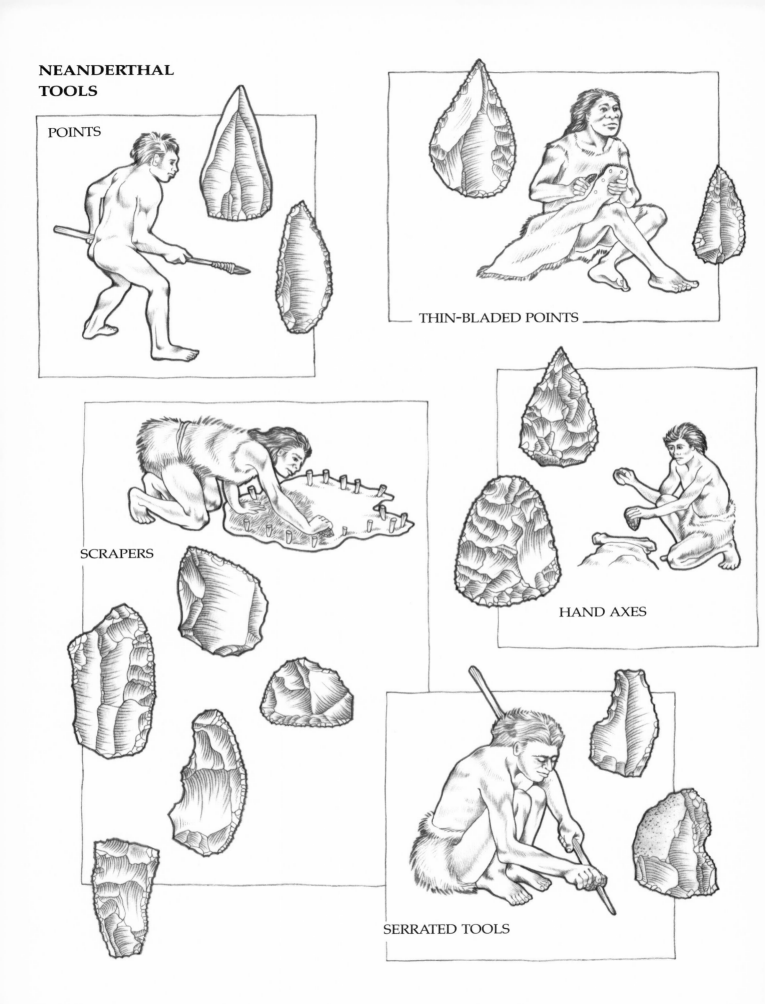

NEANDERTHAL TOOLS

POINTS

THIN-BLADED POINTS

SCRAPERS

HAND AXES

SERRATED TOOLS

as they worked, each member of the archaeological team might have heard echoes from long-hushed voices and imagined the movements of the Neanderthal people as they practiced their early religion.

What seemed like arrangements of bear bones were found in caves throughout Europe and parts of Asia. Scientists hypothesized the existence of a ritual focused on bears. At the end of the last ice age, there lived an enormous species of bear called the cave bear, which was similar to Alaskan Kodiak bears of today. They stood eight feet tall and could weigh up to 1,500 pounds. These bears roamed over Europe and parts of northern Asia. Formidable opponents, the bears were hunted for their meat and skin. The arrangements of bones found in the caves make it easy to believe that these animals were held in high regard by the Neanderthals, whether or not it can ever be proved that they figured in some special rite.

A single shaft of light pierces the cave. The skull of a bear rests on a grid of bones from two other bears. An old man approaches the skull. He hobbles painfully. His right arm hangs withered and lifeless by his side. In his left hand, which is gnarled with arthritis, he clenches the short bone from the leg of a bear. He stops in front of the skull. He half-sings a long string of blunt-sounding words. He inserts the leg bone through the bear skull. The chant is picked up by the other members of the band.

There are a few children here between ten and twelve years old. It is their first time. One of them, a young girl, stands in the deepest shadows. She is caught in a blur of fear and wonder, for it seems to her as if things, everyday things—the objects, the people she has always known—have been oddly transformed. The people stare without seeing. They sing without hearing. Their eyes, like the bear's sockets, seem empty yet knowing. And now she is expected to learn this ceremony. She wishes she were not in this cave. Anywhere else, but not this cave!

She used to think that the most frightening thing in the world was her dream of accidentally walking into the territory of a cave lion. In her dream the lion picked up her scent and waited, crouching, ready to spring. She always woke up just as it screeched, feeling its warm, rank breath washing over her. But now she knows something even more terrifying—a dream from which she may never awake.

Then something begins to change. In her dream of the lion she was always alone. But now she can feel her own people surrounding her with their strength. She waits, and listens, and begins to see that they are not strangers to her after all and that soon she will know them and they will know her in a new, more powerful way. This is no bad dream. It is a vision of the future, and it is real. She can see it in the open-eyed sleep of the others, in the depth of their trance. And she can see it in the empty sockets of the cave bear's eyes. And now she can see it in herself. Now she is the one crouching, ready to spring into her own new life.

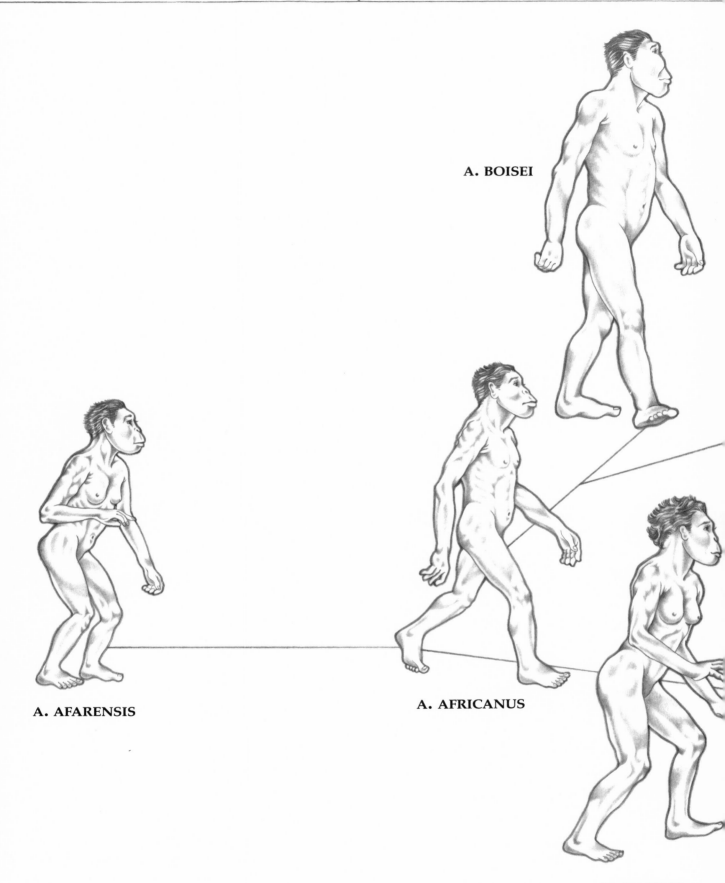

A. BOISEI

A. AFARENSIS

A. AFRICANUS

H. HABILIS

THE EVOLUTIONARY PATH

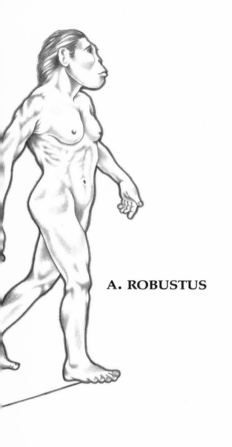

A. ROBUSTUS

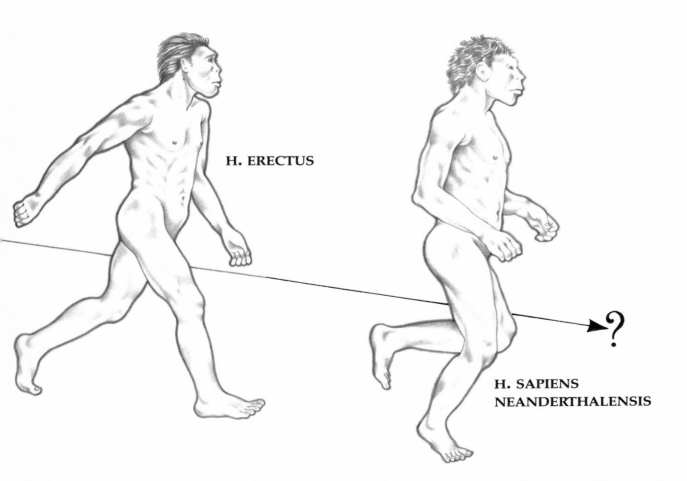

H. ERECTUS

H. SAPIENS
NEANDERTHALENSIS

Today, among certain Siberian peoples and the Ainus of northern Japan, bears are held captive in caves and then ceremonially killed at the end of winter. It is believed that the spirit of the bear then joins with the spirit of the forest god to ensure good hunting for the following year. It is not hard to theorize that the evidence found in the Neanderthals' caves was connected to similar rituals of hunting.

Some will call such practices "hunting magic." Some will call them "religious." Whether the practices are considered religion or magic, the bones of the cave bear, along with the ancient graves, point to humankind's burgeoning awareness of a world beyond material things, a timeless world of the spirit. And yet *Homo sapiens neanderthalensis* were quite different from what we with our narrow view would consider to be modern human beings.

The Neanderthal people present a riddle in the evolution of humankind, for they lived and died out within a period of 95,000 years, a very short span when compared to other hominids. Were they less suited to survive? Were they too specialized for the cold weather and unable to adapt to the warming trend as the ice age retreated? Nobody knows precisely why they became extinct. Some suppose Neanderthals were killed by the Cro-Magnons, a more modern species of humans. Or perhaps the two groups interbred until the Neanderthals were absorbed. But there is simply no evidence to support any one theory. About 35,000 years ago the Neanderthals disappeared.

Much of the incredible story of humankind has been learned through the fossil record of bones and stone implements. It is odd, then, that something as fragile as a grave could provide our first real glimpse into early people's feelings. In the shadow of the burial sites at Shanidar and La Chapelle aux Saints,   the differences between ourselves and our ancestors temporarily vanish and we feel a new kinship with a people who grieved and felt loss in much the same way we do. Through those early stirrings of human emotion a gulf of 100,000 years can be closed.

The First Modern Human Beings

There is a cave in the southwest of France called Font de Gaume. The entrance is under a large cliff overhang. Just beyond the entrance the cave divides into three branches.

It is 30,000 years ago. Along one of the branches, at a point deep within the cave, there can be seen a small pool of light and there is the odor of burning animal fat. A young man is studying the cave wall. He runs his hand over the surface, sensitive to the texture of the rock. With his fingertips he

traces the stalactite formations that wrinkle the surface of the rock. Within a narrow space there are several stalactites that have gouged deeply.

What sinew, he thinks, they would provide for a leaping horse. If he were to arrange his drawing so that the hindquarters started here—he measures it out roughly with his hands as he begins to plan the placement of the horse—then the forelegs, which will be off the ground, will be here where the rock is the smoothest. And right at the point where the forelegs join the body the rock ripples once again with stalactites. Perfect for the shoulder muscles! From a soft leather pouch hanging from his belt he takes a piece of charcoal and begins to sketch in the rough outline of the leaping horse. He sees muscle where there is only rock. He holds an image of action in the stillness of a dark cave. He fits his concept of a leaping horse to the "canvas" of the rock wall in order to express an essence of life. He is an artist.

He is among the first of the modern human beings, *Homo sapiens sapiens*, to live in Europe. For roughly two million years before him, all hominids of the *Homo* line are called "archaic," meaning that they come from an earlier or more primitive time. These include *Homo erectus* and the archaic *Homo sapiens*, among which were the Neanderthals.

Modern *Homo sapiens* came on the scene about 90,000 years ago. The first fossil bones of these people to be discovered were in the cave of Cro-Magnon near the village of Les Eyzies in France and dated at twenty-five to thirty thousand years old. There were many similar fossils

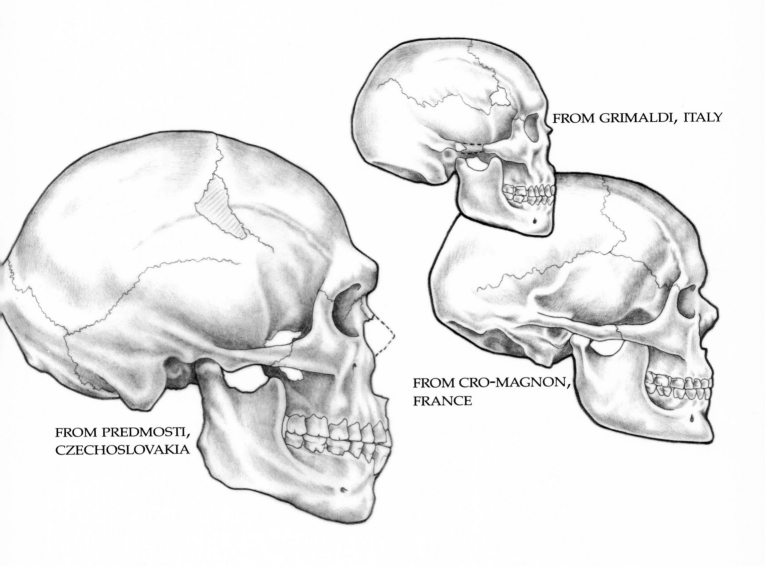

FROM GRIMALDI, ITALY

FROM CRO-MAGNON,
FRANCE

FROM PREDMOSTI,
CZECHOSLOVAKIA

discovered in other parts of the world, some of them dated much earlier.

The foreheads of the Cro-Magnons are vertical and no longer sloped; their skulls are higher and domed, not flat. The faces are smaller than those of any of the hominids that came before. The Cro-Magnon people were almost identical to ourselves. Compared to the Neanderthals they were taller but of less rugged build. Their brains in relation to their body size were larger than those of any other previous hominids. We know of their skills and intelligence not simply from fossilized skulls but

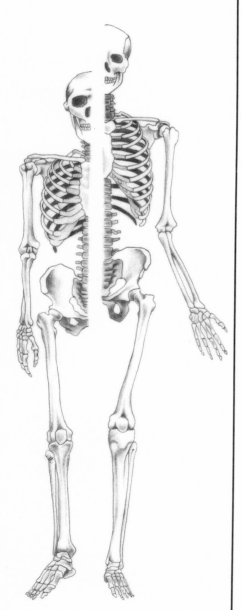

NEANDERTHAL   CRO-MAGNON

from the many stone tools in the archaeological record.

A wealth of statistics has been gathered from excavated caves and campsites that tell us a great deal about the Cro-Magnon people. They sometimes lived in large bands that included from fifty to seventy-five people. A more complex social structure must have evolved in order for such large numbers to live together successfully. They traded with other groups far away. This is known because such trading items as seashells have been found at sites that are nowhere near the sea. The Cro-Magnons did not often live in caves but set up seasonal camps for special purposes—for following game herds or for protection from winter storms.

The roots of *Homo sapiens sapiens* have been traced to Africa, where there is evidence of part modern, part archaic humans as far back as 125,000 years. A recent fossil discovery in a cave in Israel has revealed modern human beings living there as long ago as 92,000 years. These finds provide further proof that modern human beings evolved in Africa, rather than independently in several places all over the world. It also suggests that they did not descend from Neanderthals who lived in Europe and Asia, for modern human beings were occupying southwest Asia long before Neanderthals arrived in that region.

Modern hominids began to spread out of Africa over tens of thousands of years. Some may have crossed to North and South America by a land bridge or even by boat. These first modern humans lived in Europe about 35,000 to 10,000 years ago in a period of time known as the Upper Paleolithic. Another ice age had come, and they adapted well to it. The tool kit of the Cro-Magnon people was widely varied. The stoneworkers had become more specialized and could produce many kinds of blades of

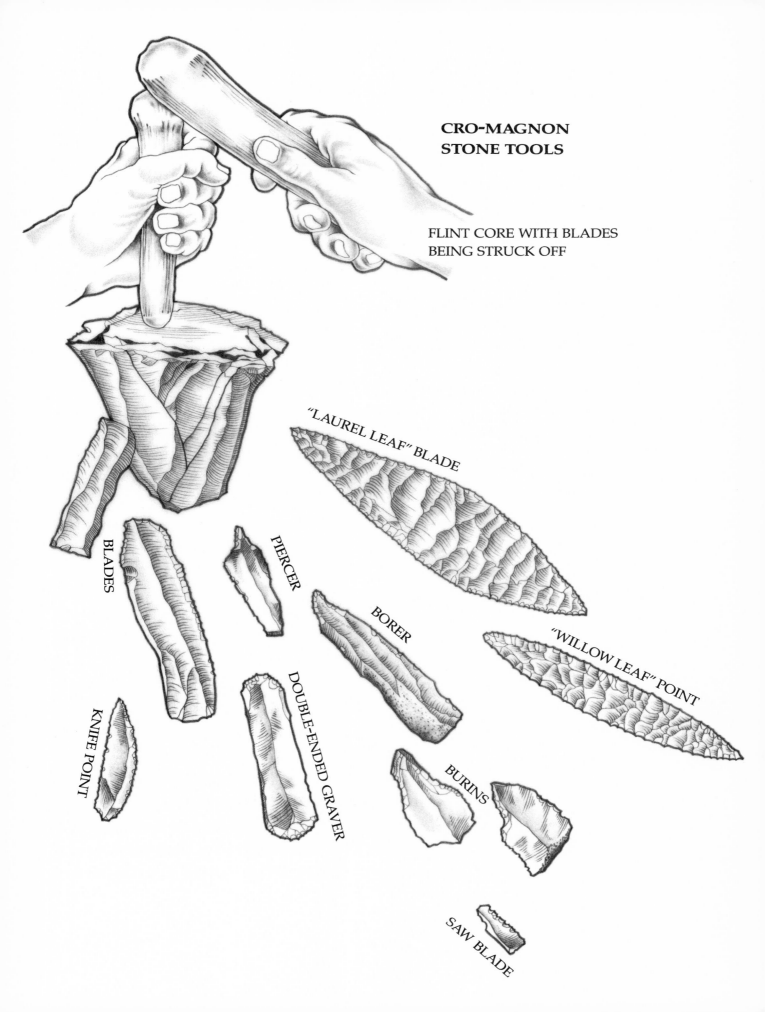

CRO-MAGNON
STONE TOOLS

FLINT CORE WITH BLADES
BEING STRUCK OFF

"LAUREL LEAF" BLADE

BLADES

PIERCER

BORER

"WILLOW LEAF" POINT

KNIFE POINT

DOUBLE-ENDED GRAVER

BURINS

SAW BLADE

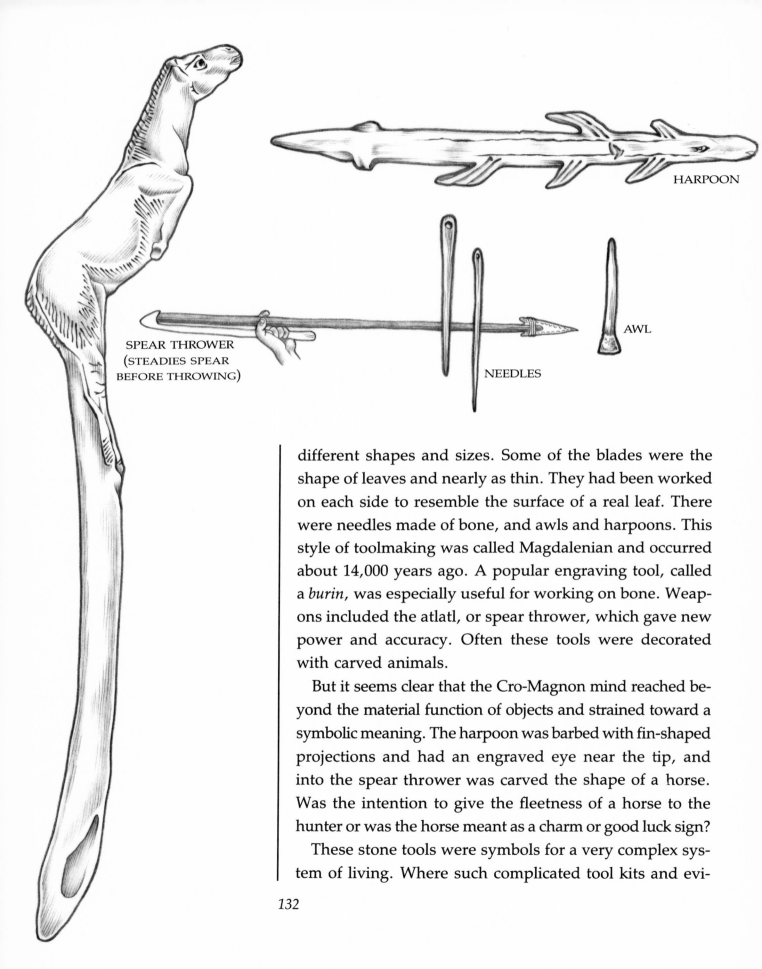

SPEAR THROWER
(STEADIES SPEAR
BEFORE THROWING)

HARPOON

NEEDLES

AWL

different shapes and sizes. Some of the blades were the shape of leaves and nearly as thin. They had been worked on each side to resemble the surface of a real leaf. There were needles made of bone, and awls and harpoons. This style of toolmaking was called Magdalenian and occurred about 14,000 years ago. A popular engraving tool, called a *burin*, was especially useful for working on bone. Weapons included the atlatl, or spear thrower, which gave new power and accuracy. Often these tools were decorated with carved animals.

But it seems clear that the Cro-Magnon mind reached beyond the material function of objects and strained toward a symbolic meaning. The harpoon was barbed with fin-shaped projections and had an engraved eye near the tip, and into the spear thrower was carved the shape of a horse. Was the intention to give the fleetness of a horse to the hunter or was the horse meant as a charm or good luck sign?

These stone tools were symbols for a very complex system of living. Where such complicated tool kits and evidence of symbols have been found, we must assume that there was some form of language to communicate the experience of making and using the tools. There must have been some sort of organized social system through which to pass on cultural traditions.

For a period of time the Neanderthals and the Cro-Magnon people overlapped. There was space for both kinds of human beings to live. But the differences between Neanderthals and Cro-Magnon people were much greater than any that separate human beings today. The Neanderthals were perhaps an evolutionary side branch, a small twig on the tree of life. But the Cro-Magnon people went on. By 10,000 years ago they had begun to live in villages and to farm, as did similar people in other parts of the world.

It is so easy to look for simple explanations for why one species persists and another fades into extinction. This one stood up. That one stayed in the trees. This one was built for long hard trekking. That one could not go so far. This one could make tools and better weapons. That one had to scavenge. As a species we *Homo sapiens sapiens* have lived the shortest time of all the hominids—perhaps a mere 90,000 years. Australopithecines and hominids like *Homo erectus* flourished for a million years or more. So it would seem extremely foolish of us to look for a single reason for why we have "made it" when our species has hardly begun. But we can look back at the Cro-Magnons for signs of a kind of life that has come to have special meaning for us as human beings. It is a life that includes language, community, and a sense of imagination. There have been many treasures in the course of human evolution and this was the treasure we inherited from the Cro-Magnons, our closest ancestors in time.

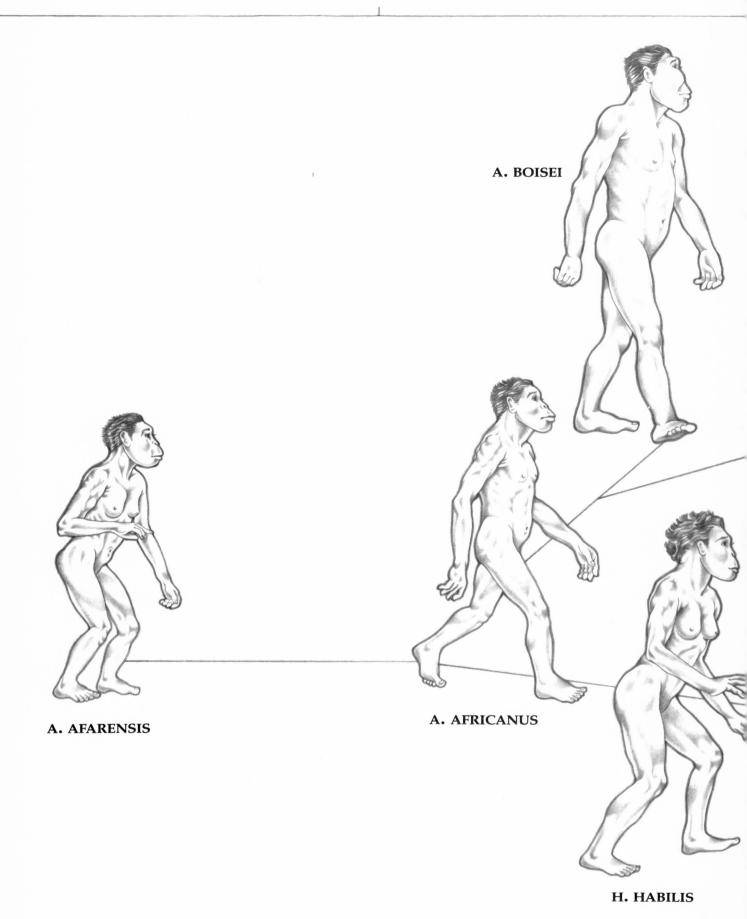

A. BOISEI

A. AFARENSIS

A. AFRICANUS

H. HABILIS

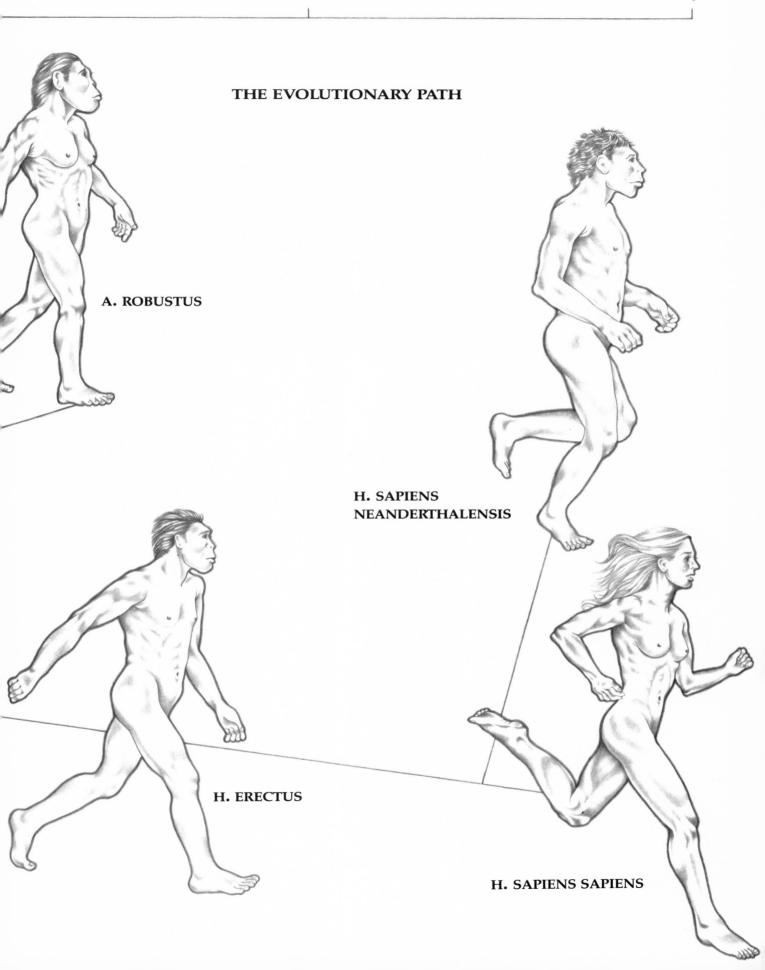

1 MYA   0

THE EVOLUTIONARY PATH

A. ROBUSTUS

H. SAPIENS
NEANDERTHALENSIS

H. ERECTUS

H. SAPIENS SAPIENS

Broderick Olcott Presides

It is the year 2,001,988.

There is a laboratory. It is not in the basement of a museum in Cleveland but in a classroom in the Pacific Rift University on the island of California. The distinguished paleoanthropologist is not Donald Johanson but Broderick Olcott, director of SPCRA—the Search for Pre-Continental Rift Ancestors. It is the first day of the new semester. A group of students awaits his introductory lecture. This lecture has to be lively enough to snag their interest, even though to many of the students some of the material is old hat. Professor Olcott needs new recruits for the field season next term if he is to get down to a very promising stratum that should contain a treasure trove of fossils from the late Holocene, the last epoch of the Cenozoic era that ended two million years ago.

Olcott is known for his artistic laser and holograph lectures. He enters the room with a flourish. There is a gasp, a wave of giggles. He is dressed in a very bizarre Holocene outfit. A faded blue fabric sheathes his legs. The front closes vertically over the pelvis with a peculiar interlocking metal mechanism. His torso is covered with a light-colored fabric; stitched above the breast is a tiny extinct creature. A girl in the front row squints slightly to get a better look. "It's an alligator," she slip-thinks—too late to close down her telesensors!

"Correct!" booms Olcott. "And would you believe," he continues, "that late Holocene hominids often used these reptilian skins for containers and shoes? They're becoming quite prevalent in the archaeological record. The shoes and the bags more than the beasts, actually."

With that remark the lights dim and the show begins. A holographic image of the Great Basalt Flow looms up. "As you know," Olcott begins with a mixture of telepathic and vocal communication, "a million and a half years or so ago, before the California Plate broke free from the

PACIFIC
RIFT
UNIVERSITY

North American Plate, there was a series of geological events that speeded along the natural movement of the earth. One of the most catastrophic of these was the First Great Ooze of 1.25 million years ago when a steady stream of lava squeezed out of a rift in the seafloor, covered twenty percent of the North American Plate, and gave the old heave-ho to what was once known as the Arctic Circle. Now what did our late Holocene ancestors do? Sit there and evolve? No, of course not. They moved. In the Pleistocene we had the great ice ages. In the Holocene the great oozes occurred with some regularity. The times in between were called the interoozials."

The hologram shifts but Professor Olcott flashes a telepathic footnote to the students to note the fossil print in the basalt of the alligator handbag. His lectures are masterpieces, weaving together telepathic thought, vocal language, and holographic images. True multimedia experiences.

"It was in these interoozial periods," he continues, "that we saw the rapid evolutionary changes in *Homo sapiens sapiens* that led us to *Homo sapiens sapiens sapiens*, or *Homo telepathicus*, or, as we are popularly known, 'Triple Saps.' There is, however, a great gap in the fossil record. It is almost as if one of these *Homo sapiens sapiens* of the Holocene—" There is a loud roar of laughter as Olcott flashes a joke to the class of an early *Homo sapiens sapiens* taking a dive into a Holocene Hole and then coming out a Triple Sap.

"We know it was not that simple," he continues after the laughter subsides. "But our mission here

138

is to try and figure out what was in that gap. We are learning more with our laser excavations of the various basalt archipelagoes of the Old New England Plate and the Great Basin and various other sites around the globe. What we want to find out is, who was this creature who stood at the fork in the road between the Double Saps and the Triple Saps, between *Homo sapiens sapiens* and *Homo telepathicus*? Suzanne Greenspoon's extraordinary find, two summers ago, of this intriguing specimen offers our most complete skull and brain fossils to date.''

There is a gasp as the skull looms in holographic dimensions. ''This is Peggy Sue, named for the comet that we have seen every thirty-six years for the past three centuries. This holographic image, by the way, appeared in the most recent *National Geographic* laser disc. Yes, it's the one with the cover story on the group of dolphins that have finally been trained to program computers.

''Well, getting back to Peggy Sue. We want to know more about her. Was *she* the last common ancestor we shared with the Double Saps?''

Professor Olcott can feel the students falling into the age-old trap of comparing all previous hominids to themselves and concluding that they are the smartest and the most advanced. He can feel their collective thought: PRIMITIVE. He stops and sighs deeply. ''She is our last great mystery.'' He pauses again. ''You know, in our telepathic world there are so few real mysteries. But in the pretelepathic era there was a time when art and music and vocal language could not be so easily understood. They had to be pondered, and wondered about, and discussed in greater depth. So do not dismiss Peggy Sue as a mere primitive being. She was special. Her time was special. It was a time when meaning was sometimes hidden and pictures were incomplete. It was a time of *books*—" Professor Olcott's voice is choked with emotion as he gazes back two million years— "and a time for slow wonder and imagination."

Notes

CHAPTER TWO

Pages 17–19/ Readers interested in learning more about Donald Johanson's discovery can read the Prologue to *Lucy: The Beginnings of Humankind* (see Selected Bibliography).

CHAPTER FOUR

Pages 31–32/ These verses are taken from Alexander Pope's *Essay on Man*, excerpts from which can be found in many poetry anthologies.

Pages 38–39/ The final quotation in this chapter is from Charles Darwin's *Descent of Man* and can be found on page 199 of the Princeton University Press edition (1981). An accessible treatment of Darwin's theories is available in *Darwin for Beginners* (see Selected Bibliography).

CHAPTER FIVE

Pages 50–51/ These quotations are from Dr. David Pilbeam's "Rethinking Human Origins," *Discovery Magazine* (Yale–Peabody Museum), Vol. 13, No. 1, 1978, pp. 2–9.

CHAPTER SIX

Page 53/ Mary Leakey writes of her discovery of the Laetoli footprints in "Footprints in the Ashes of Time," *National Geographic*, Vol. 155, No. 4, April 1979, p. 453.

CHAPTER SEVEN

Quotations throughout this chapter are taken from *Adventures with the Missing Link* by Raymond A. Dart with Dennis Craig (New York: Harper & Brothers, Publishers, 1959), which is now out of print.

Page 69/ Sir Arthur Keith's dismissive comments on the Taung Child are quoted on page 45 of *Lucy: The Beginnings of Humankind* (see Selected Bibliography).

CHAPTER EIGHT

Page 77/ This quotation is taken from *Adventures with the Missing Link* (see note, Chapter Seven).

CHAPTER NINE

Page 90/ Richard H. Leakey's account of childhood journeys to Lake Victoria is taken from *One Life: An Autobiography* (Salem, New Hampshire: Salem House, 1984), p. 24.

Selected Bibliography

Many books were used by the author and the illustrator in the writing of *Traces of Life: The Origins of Humankind.* Among them were:

Darwin, Charles. *Origin of Species.* New York: Collier Books, 1962.

Edey, Maitland, and Donald Johanson. *Lucy: The Beginnings of Humankind.* New York: Warner Books, 1981.

Gowlett, John. *Ascent to Civilization: The Archaeology of Early Man.* New York: Alfred Knopf, 1984.

Leakey, Richard E., and Roger Lewin. *Origins.* New York: E. P. Dutton, 1977.

Lewin, Roger. *Bones of Contention.* New York: Simon and Schuster, 1987.

———. *Human Evolution, an Illustrated Introduction.* New York: W. H. Freeman & Co., 1984.

———. *Thread of Life: The Smithsonian Looks at Evolution.* Washington, D.C.: Smithsonian Books, 1982.

Malatesta, Anne, and Ronald Friedland. *The White Kikuyu: Louis B. Leakey.* New York: McGraw-Hill, 1978.

*Miller, Jonathan, and Borin Van Loon. *Darwin For Beginners.* New York: Pantheon Books, 1982.

*Zihlman, Adrienne L. *The Human Evolution Coloring Book.* New York: Barnes and Noble Books (a division of Harper & Row), 1982.

*Of special interest to young readers

Index

References to illustrations or maps are in *italics*.

Aegyptopithecus ("Dawn Ape"), 42–44, *42*, *48–49*
Ainu people, 124
algae, 6
Amud, *116*
apes, 32–44, 48–49, 75
archaeologists, 21, 23, 26, 78
Australopithecus (australopithecines), 14, *15*, *58*, *59*, 103, *133*
Australopithecus afarensis, 56–62, *56*, *61*, *75*, *76*, *134*
Australopithecus africanus, 67, 72, 74–76, *76*, 91, 93, *134*
Australopithecus boisei, 76–84, *76*, *78*, *80–83*, *134*
Australopithecus robustus, 76, *76*, *78*, 103, *135*
Awash River, *21*

bacteria, 4
Beagle, HMS, 33–37, *34–35*
biochemical studies, 49–50

blood proteins, 49–50
Blue Nile, *21*
Boise, Charles, 76
brain capacity, 93–94
branching, 40–41, *41*
Broken Hill archaic skull, *102*, *108*
Broom, Robert, 75
burials, 112–14, 124–25
burins, 132

Cambrian Explosion, 6–8, *6*
camp, 25–28, *26–27*
cartographers (mapmakers), 21, *27*
cataloguers, *27*, 28
cave bears, 117–21, *121*, 124
cave drawings, 126–28, *127*
chimpanzees, *16–17*, 42, 50, *59*, 67, 75
"Cindy" (fossil remains), 90–93, *90*
conservators, *26–27*
continents, movement of, 7–8, *7*
Cooke, Basil, 22–23, 29
cooks, *27*, 28
Cro-Magnons, 124, *127*, 128–33, *129–32*
Czechoslovakia, *129*

Dart, Raymond, 64–72, *65*, 74, 77, 99
Darwin, Charles, 32–39, *32*, *38*, 41–42, 66, 96, 97
dating, 27, 28–29, 91
"Dawn Ape," *See Aegyptopithecus*
Dawson, Charles, 69
"Denkenesh" (other name for "Lucy"), 19
dinosaurs, 8–10, *8*
Drachenloch cave, 117–19
Dryopithecus (Proconsul), 44, *44*, *48–49*
Dubois, Eugene, 97–99, *97*

East Turkana, 92
Eoanthropus dawsoni, 69
Ethiopia, 13, 18–19, *21*, 25, 56, 57
excavators, 21, 25

faking a skull, *70–71*
fire, 103
"First Family," 57
FitzRoy, Robert, 33
Font de Gaume cave, 126–28

143